LEADERS
MARCHING
FORWARD

LEADERS MARCHING FORWARD

FRED GROOMS

THE ADVANCED STUDENT LEADERSHIP FIELD MANUAL

Barnabas Consulting LLC
Blythewood, South Carolina

Barnabas Consulting LLC
Blythewood, South Carolina
www.fredgrooms.com

ISBN 978-0-9914628-7-2 (paperback)
ISBN 978-0-9914628-8-9 (Kindle ebook)

Printed in the United States of America

Editing by Cathy Reed, www.cathyreedediting.com
Cover design by Brian J. Halley, www.bookcreatives.com
Interior design by Jennifer Omner, www.allpublications.com

Contents

Preface

I'd like to thank you for selecting *Leaders Marching Forward: The Advanced Student Leadership Field Manual*. This book is designed as a companion to my bestselling student leadership book, *B.A.S.I.C. The Student Leadership Field Manual: Leadership Lessons For Every Student*, which teaches the foundational elements of leadership.

Leaders Marching Forward: The Advanced Student Leadership Field Manual is designed to teach students the next level of leadership skills. It is not essential for you to read *B.A.S.I.C.* before you read *Leaders Marching Forward* because the information in this book can stand alone. However, I would suggest that you *do* read *B.A.S.I.C.*, or at least pick up a copy, so you can keep both books as references in your leadership library. As your leadership opportunities advance, it is vital that you continue to gain knowledge and skills as a leader. *Leaders Marching Forward* is the perfect choice to assist you in becoming not just a good leader but an exceptional leader, a leader that others *choose* to follow.

Purpose

In the pages that follow, you will find a proven approach to student leadership that will help you develop your personal and professional leadership skills. This approach is based upon the US Army's leadership philosophy. This historically proven leadership model has given seemingly average young men and women the greatest opportunity to become superior leaders, more than any other leadership model. It is a philosophy that has been battle-tested over time and proven to work in a wide range of circumstances.

With this philosophy in mind, using the official Army Leadership Field Manual, and based on my personal leadership experiences as a veteran Army Officer and seasoned leadership trainer, I have created the advanced leadership training. I have taken the Army leadership training program and molded it in such a way that it is student-friendly. The reader will not find 'war stories' within the pages of this book; in this context, they are neither necessary nor appropriate.

$$\bullet \ \bullet \ \bullet$$

It is important to note that my goal is not to recruit you or anyone else to become a member of the military. The military is right only for a very few; and joining the military is a personal decision, a decision not made quickly or without the support of family and friends.

The Army has a long history of producing great leaders, and the Army leadership model is known to be a superior leadership training system. The military counts among its finest leaders: presidents, lawmakers, astronauts, CEO's, teachers, professors, and leaders in every other civilian career. Less than three percent of the US population will ever serve in the military, yet those who do are highly sought after for their leadership training and advanced leadership skills.

The military philosophy of leadership is often misunderstood. When people think about military leadership, they often envision an officer or sergeant standing before their unit shouting orders to the soldiers. They then assume that those soldiers blindly follow these orders as if they were robots, never asking questions and never having input. This couldn't be further from the truth.

Also, people often think that military leadership is built around fear and intimidation. This is enormously inaccurate. If one were to think military leadership is solely about rank, they would also be wrong. At its very core, military leadership is about building individual character, resilience, trust and cooperation. It also includes the highest level of training possible, shared experiences, personal skills, and accountability. Unlike civilian organizations that will wait for you to prove your leadership ability, the Army believes you're a leader unless you prove otherwise, and then the Army will work on developing the leadership skills you are missing. The military is not satisfied if you're not continually advancing your leadership skills.

As mentioned earlier, I use the Army model, and in a greater sense the military model, of leadership as the backdrop for my leadership training. While the Army's Leadership Field Manual is a superior training tool, it makes an assumption that we *cannot* make with this leadership field manual that I have written, and that is: it assumes you are in the Army, and it assumes you have been through *basic training*, the very first step in the process of becoming an Army leader.

For the purposes of understanding how the Army's leadership method applies to you, I have created the acronym **B.A.S.I.C.** Each element of the acronym **B.A.S.I.C.** was unpacked in my first book—which I recommend that you read first.

B.A.S.I.C.

B. Behavior: What you do matters as you lead yourself and others.

A. Attitude: What you think and how you respond is always within your control.

S. Skills: What you do and how well you do it increases your value.

I. Integrity: What you regard as right and true is demonstrated in your character.

C. Choices: What you choose affects your future success.

Now you will need to start developing your intermediate and advanced leadership skills.

Part One: Next Level Leadership
   Self-Leadership
   Developing a Team
   Commitment
   Time Management

Part Two: Marching Onward
   Communication
   Morale
   Evaluation
   Shortening the Learning Curve: Mentoring and Coaching
   Becoming a Resilient Leader

Introduction

Some individuals reading this book will not have read my first book *B.A.S.I.C. The Student Leadership Field Manual: Leadership Lessons for Every Student.* I would like to encourage you to do so prior to reading this book. However, if you feel you are ready for some advanced training as a young leader, please go ahead.

But let's not assume we are ready to continue just yet, or that we don't not need a quick refresher before continuing. It's vital that we establish some basic understanding about leadership before we proceed.

First, leadership is inevitable. At some point, you will be leading your peer group, team, tribe, employees, friends or family. Every group, job or organization of which you will be a member has some form of leadership requirement. As you progress in your career or careers, you will be leading others. Many of you are already leading others in official roles and that's why you have selected *Leaders Marching Forward*.

Leadership is a skill, and since it is a skill, leadership can be taught, learned and invested in. Over time, as you invest in the skill of leadership, you can move towards mastering this skill. Once you begin to master the skill of leadership, you become highly valuable. When you become highly valuable, you become highly sought after. When you are highly sought after, you have more control over your future. Who doesn't want more control over their future? So it is vital that you start developing the skill of leadership today rather than tomorrow.

Leadership Defined

Leadership is the art and science of influencing others. It is the means by which you get people to accomplish a mission, task or goal. More simply put, leadership is about you influencing others to get stuff done.

As a student leader, it becomes your responsibility to develop your ability to influence others. You must learn that leadership takes personal responsibility and accountability, and that it takes personal and moral courage. As a leader, you open yourself to criticism, conflict, and questioning. People will push back at your leadership and criticize you personally. They will question every decision you make, especially as you advance in responsibility.

Plus, you will be navigating in a leadership landscape that is rapidly changing; you are going to face leadership challenges no generation has ever faced before. You are going to have to possess a level of confidence in your ability to lead yourself well before you are able to lead others effectively.

Leaders Marching Forward: The Advanced Student Leadership Field Manual is your next level of leadership training. As a young soldier in the Army, once you have graduated basic training, you then move on to your Advanced Individual Training, also known as AIT. This book is your AIT.

In this book, I'll provide an essential introduction to advanced leadership skills. Each skill could have, and in most cases does have, entire books devoted to it. My goal is to help you learn to define the skill and employ it in your leadership skill set. I would also encourage you, over time, to seek out additional resources on each skill that we discuss in this book.

Developing your leadership skills is a lifelong endeavor, so never stop learning.

Section One: Next Level Leadership unpacks the leadership skills you will face right after taking on the role of leader. These skills include: Self-leadership, Developing a Team, Commitment, and Time Management.

In Section Two: Marching Onward, we'll cover leadership skills that you will also need to develop quickly after assuming your leadership role. These include: Communication, Morale, Evaluation, and Shortening the Learning Curve. Plus, I have included a bonus chapter on becoming a Resilient Leader.

Leaders Marching Forward

In many of my keynote speeches, I start by teaching the audience to do what is known as a "mark time march." It works like this: the audience is asked to stand and place their hands at their sides, and to place the heels of their feet together at a forty-five degree angle. Then on my command of "forward march," everyone steps off on their left foot and marches (hopefully) in step together: "left right, left right, left right, left." Then once we are in step marching in place, I call out a cadence and the audience returns that cadence in response.

A sample cadence

Me: There's nowhere else I'd rather be
Audience: There's nowhere else I'd rather be

Me: Than here making history
Audience: Than here making history

Me: Leadership's the life for me
Audience: Leadership's the life for me.

This is great fun, especially when the crowd is large and we can make a huge amount of noise. Often times we are not all that successful at getting everyone in step, but what is most important is the lesson everyone learns. And that is: It is the leader's responsibility to move individuals, groups, and teams *forward*. As a leader, it is your responsibility to move your organization *forward* towards the mission, tasks, and goals set before you.

Before we can move an individual soldier forward, we have to get them to march in place. They have to know their left foot from their right foot. Once they do, we then place a recruit to their left and a recruit to their right. Then they march in place until they can stay in step together. Next they are given the command to march forward while staying in step as a unit. It's their leader's responsibility to teach this basic principle, and soldiers must master this rudimentary task within minutes.

Army leadership is founded upon basic or foundational elements like the mark time march. Marching as an individual is expanded to marching as a squad of 11–15; then to a platoon of 4 squads; then to a company of 4 platoons; and then to a battalion of 4–6 companies. This continues to expand out to moving thousands of soldiers to tens of thousands of soldiers, and hundreds of billions of dollars worth of equipment and supplies, all over the world rapidly. None of this is possible unless a soldier's leadership teaches them how to mark time march.

As a leader it is your responsibility to teach your organization to march forward towards success. It all starts with one step at a time.—*Illustration 1*

Part One

Next Level Leadership

Section One

Self-Leadership

1-1-1. Once a soldier has graduated from basic training, they must immediately step up and start taking control of themselves. There is no time for hand-holding any longer. They are going to move into their Advanced Individual Training (AIT), where each soldier learns their specific job skills. Each soldier has learned what it means to be under the command of others, and now it's time that they start taking command of themselves; and their leadership expects nothing less. We call this self-leadership.

1-1-2. Self-leadership is the best first step you can take in developing your next level of leadership potential and leadership style. It's often the missing link in developing strong leadership skills. It's potentially the one area where you can self-destruct as a young leader and perhaps never recover. As a student you must learn to lead yourself before you will be able to successfully lead others. You have to develop a better grasp of whom you are and where you'd like to see yourself in the future. You need to take time to discover your true strengths and learn to manage your weaknesses. *Influence* is the key to successful leadership. So it makes sense that as a leader you have to be able to create and maintain positive influence over yourself. If you can't lead yourself, how can you expect to lead anyone else?

Don't Be Someone You're Not

Back in the 19th century, a guy by the name of Thomas Carlyle developed the "Great Man" theory. The Great Man theory assumed that *leaders are born, not made*, and that these leaders will arise when there is great need. Back when Carlyle was studying leaders, almost all leaders came from wealth and aristocracy and were, of course, men. Money equaled power and position. Thus, this promoted the notion that great leaders were from great wealth and good breeding.

One of the serious flaws in this theory was that Carlyle was only studying individuals who were already considered to be great leaders. His conclusion was that in order to be a great leader, you had to be born with the correct "leadership traits," and then you had to emulate those "natural traits" of the great leaders before you. In essence, you had to become like the leaders who were leading you in order to be successful. He was wrong.

A common mistake among young leaders is to do exactly what the Great Man theory suggests—become like the leaders before you. If their leadership style worked, it's natural to assume that the same leadership style will work for you as well. The problem is that it is unlikely your natural leadership traits are all that similar to the person whom you are replacing. So don't assume that what someone did before you will now work for you.

Fortunately, we have since become wiser than in the days of Carlyle. It may be true that some people seem to be natural born leaders (men and women), but more often than not, great leaders have *learned* to develop their leadership skills and to become *more* of who they already are, rather than attempt to be someone they are not.—*Illustration 2*

Four Core Principles for Mastering Self-Leadership

1-1-3. I'm going to give you four core principles for mastering self-leadership. Some people will suggest that there are many additional principles, but for our purposes, we will focus on just these four.

Principle One: Self-discipline

1-1-4. Let me make it clear right away that self-discipline is a learned trait. It will require sacrifice, commitment, and repetition. It is about self-control and personal motivation. Long-term success as a leader is related directly to your ability to be self-disciplined. As a young leader you have to develop a strong sense of self-discipline quickly. When you do, it will set you apart from your peers. You have to take charge of what you do, when you do it, with whom you do it, all the time.

1-1-5. It's vital that you are self-disciplined if you ever plan on achieving your goals or the goals you set for your team. According to a 2013 study by Wilhelm Hoffman, people with high self-discipline are happier than those without. The study discovered that self-disciplined subjects were more capable of dealing with goal conflicts, thus creating personal flexibility and creativity. They spent less time debating whether to indulge in behaviors detrimental to their health and were able to make positive decisions more easily. The self-disciplined subjects did not allow their choices to be driven by impulse or feelings. Instead, they made informed, rational decisions on a daily basis without feeling overly stressed or upset.

1-1-6. A key area of self-discipline in your life is your health. The military has a high standard of fitness that every soldier is required to maintain. If you don't, you can and likely will lose your job; and yes, the military can release soldiers for poor health and fitness. Being overweight and out of shape can be a real danger within the military. It's unlikely that your civilian job will have the same standards as the military, but many corporations have health incentives because of the direct benefit of having healthy employees. As the leader, you should be setting the standard for the rest of your team when it comes to health and fitness. If you're unhealthy, it's very likely your team will be unhealthy. If you maintain healthy habits, it's more likely your team will maintain healthy habits. People want to be like their leaders. So set the correct example for them to follow.

1-1-7. Self-discipline means you're less likely to indulge in behaviors that are harmful to your health, and you're more likely to make positive decisions. You don't allow yourself to make choices impulsively or based solely upon your feelings or limited experience.

1-1-8. Self-discipline is also about developing appropriate work habits, including managing your time (See 1-4-2). As a leader, showing up on time, being prepared, and being fully present while on the job is a *must*. A self-disciplined leader is the first to arrive and the last to leave. You don't ask people to do what you have not already done or are willing to do yourself. Leaders lead by example.

Principle Two: Self-awareness

1-1-9. Self-leadership is about self-awareness. Self-awareness is having high moral standards, strong values, and high quality character, all of which are hallmarks of quality leadership. I'll say it again: people pay more attention to a leader's actions than a leader's words. You have to be accountable for your actions and your reactions. Hypocrisy, i.e., saying one thing and doing another, has no place in your life if you're going to become a quality leader.

1-1-10. Self-awareness is about having identified your unique talents and invested in those talents to create your personal strength set. A leader must also identify their weaknesses and learn to manage their weaknesses.

Principle Three: Perseverance

1-1-11. Self-leadership is about perseverance and grit. Life is not fair, and life will create difficult situations. As soon as you think you have it all figured out, something or someone new will come along and cause trouble. Change is inevitable. A leader must persevere in times of conflict and difficulty. You have to be tough on the inside and on the outside. People will challenge your authority and you must be ready. Perseverance and grit are about maintaining a focused attitude of success. We'll cover perseverance in more detail in The Resilient Leader section.

Principle Four: Self-motivation

1-1-12. Self-leadership is about self-motivation. Too often we rely on others to motivate us or make us 'happy.' As a leader you have to be the one motivating others towards specific goals. Therefore, you have to be able to motivate yourself, especially on the days you would just as soon stay home or stay in bed. When you are self-motivated, you have a clear understanding of your goals and the goals of those you are leading. You focus on the solutions and outcomes, not on the problems. Self-motivation takes practice and is developed over time.

1-1-13. Being self-motivated also requires you to be a self-learner. Your education should never stop. If you stop learning, you stop advancing. If you stop advancing, your value will diminish; you will not be a valuable asset. The very best leaders are self-motivated learners. They are always seeking out new information and new challenges. Soldiers are always learning new skills; it is built into the fabric of military training and discipline. In the army, there is always a training school to attend, whether it's Airborne School or teaching you to help other soldiers do their taxes.

The Early Bird Catches the Worm

My goal as an officer was always to be the first one to arrive and the last to leave. The reason was simple: for me, it was about self-discipline. And that hasn't changed over the years, no matter what my job has been or whom I am leading.

It was one way that, as a young leader, I could demonstrate to my soldiers that I was always at the ready. It took self-discipline, perseverance, and motivation to always be the first to arrive. Yet for me, it was mostly about self-awareness. I was going to set a high standard for my troops. It was a way of letting them know that I would never ask them to do what I was not willing to do, had not been trained to do, or had not already done in the past.

This worked well as a leadership trait, until the time when I was a young Captain and I started working with Sergeant First Class (SFC) Taylor. SFC Taylor also felt the need to be the first to arrive and the last to leave. So we found ourselves trying to outdo each other. The result was that we were both unnecessarily early and stayed unnecessarily late all in an attempt to outdo one another.

So I came up with a compromise: we would take turns. Simple as that. SFC Taylor would arrive early and I would be the last to leave. We even took turns rotating being early and late.—*Illustration 3*

Section Two

Developing a Team

1-2-1. Now that you have a good idea of what it means to be able to lead yourself; it's time to develop your team. You have to ask yourself: What should my team look like? Who should I recruit to be on my team? What kind of skills do I need them to have? A leader who can develop the right team can easily set themselves apart and move from being a good leader to being a great leader.

1-2-2. Before you start developing your own team, you have to remember that your job, as the leader within an organization, is to influence others to accomplish the mission, task or goals set for you by those who are leading *you*. Remember, even though we are talking about advanced leadership skills, you are likely not the *boss* running the organization just yet. This is probably your first time developing your own leadership team, and your team has to focus on the goals and vision set for you by those whom *you* are following.

1-2-3. I'd encourage you to read or reread Part One and Part Two from my first book: *B.A.S.I.C. The Student Leadership Field Manual.* Meanwhile, here is a short reminder of that information. In order to *be* in command, you must first learn to *come under* command. Learning to come under command is something that all successful leaders must do, but placing yourself under someone's command is not always easy, especially when you are young and you are just starting to feel yourself gaining some independence. But being under command is not about surrendering your independence; it is about gaining your *future* independence. One of the most important aspects of the military model of leadership is that every soldier, no matter their rank, is both a leader and a subordinate at the same time. They are both in command and under command, and this creates a mutual respect for each other. No leader is better than the subordinates he or she is leading.

1-2-4. This is precisely where you are now. You have come under the command of the leadership over you, and now it's time for you to start leading others. Your first big step is to create a team that can implement the vision, decisions and goals of your superiors.

Surround Yourself with People Who Are Smarter than You

1-2-5. "Surround yourself with people who are smarter than you and take credit for what they do." This was the advice given to me by a retired Lieutenant Colonel (LTC) who had an outstanding military career. The advice was offered the day I was commissioned as an officer, and the LTC issuing me this advice was J. R. Grooms, my father. Take time to read his advice again: "Surround yourself with people who are smarter than you and take credit for what they do." At first glance this advice seems harsh, arrogant, and just wrong, but it's actually *brilliant* advice. My father would continue to explain what he meant by this advice; and we'll get there in just a moment....

1-2-6. When you take on your first leadership position where you are responsible for developing your own leadership team, you will typically recruit from those you know best, and you will be setting yourself up for failure. Why? Because those you know best are the people who are like you in most every way. If you develop a leadership team or recruit team members that are more like you than not, your team will be clones and you will feel safe. Your friends will most likely agree with you because they think just like you; so you are less likely to run into push-back and criticism, at least at first. However, you will have difficulty with making tough decisions, being innovative, solving problems, and all manner of other issues. Don't make this mistake; you have to develop *a diverse team of people.* A team that has many different personalities, different view-points, and different cultures is a team that has the potential to excel and take you from good to great.

1-2-7. "Surround yourself with people who are smarter than you." My father was well aware of my greatest weakness—my dyslexia. He knew that if I wasn't careful, it could create many different kinds of problems for me as a young officer. What he was telling me, and what I'm telling you, is that you have to know what your weaknesses are. You have to be humble enough to know where you are going to need assistance, and you need to find people who can support your weakest areas. As a dyslexic, I had to have people on my leadership team who had the ability to assist me with grammar, spelling and my written communications. And that has not changed in all these years. It's my reality. It's my greatest weakness and I've learned to manage it. What is your greatest weakness?

1-2-8. It can be very humbling to do the self-evaluation process necessary to embrace your weaknesses. Most of us are aware of what our weaknesses are, but to admit them can be diffi-cult. The key here is that you don't have to *fix* your weaknesses. You only have to *manage* them by surrounding yourself with people who are smarter than you in your areas of weakness. My father's advice was brilliant.

1-2-9. Also, we all have prejudices or biases of some kind. As a leader you need to own those for yourself. You don't have to broadcast them; you just need to know what they are and take ownership of them. We live in an increasingly diverse nation. We are not always going to see eye to eye, and that's totally okay. But we all have to learn to get along with each other. As a young leader, make sure your team is diverse. Find people who challenge you in your areas of bias, and place at least one on your team. They will make you smarter because they will expand your own thought process.

What Now, Troy?

I led a student ministry for 15 years. During that time I had a lot of people come and go on my volunteer leadership team. But one person on my team for years was a man named Troy. Troy and I don't think alike in most areas. Troy is a very analytical thinker; he sees most things in terms of black and white, and there is little room for gray areas. He also has an uncanny ability to see issues that could cause problems, issues that no one else can see. Troy drove me crazy for years.

We'd be in a planning meeting and Troy would raise his hand, and I would immediately think to myself: "What now, Troy?" He was notorious for asking me questions that I didn't have answers to, and to be honest, it was very frustrating. It wasn't him asking questions that was frustrating; most of his questions were valid and on point. But when you're leading a team and a team member is *always* asking you questions about stuff you haven't thought of but should have, it's frustrating. This is especially true when you don't have good answers to their questions. Troy kept me on my toes all the time. I would try to anticipate his analytical thought process and be ready with really good answers. But inevitably I'd find myself thinking: "What now, Troy?"

Troy made me a better leader. He forced me to think differently and to be better prepared. Because of Troy, I would have to pay attention to areas that I might not have paid any attention to before working with him. Today, Troy has become one of my best friends.

—*Illustration 4*

1-2-10. If you hate public speaking, then make sure you have someone on your team who loves it. If you are not super creative, find people who are. If you hate dealing with numbers, find someone who's in love with accounting and get them on your team. If you love dealing with details, find others who are big picture thinkers and have them help you expand your outlook. All of these are ways that you can "surround yourself with people who are smarter than you."

1-2-11. "Surround yourself with people who are smarter than you." Let's sum up this statement.

As the leader, you need to create a team that covers your weakest areas, so that your strengths shine through. Find people who know stuff you don't. Place individuals on your team who will challenge your thinking. All of this makes you smarter. Then remember that your team's successes and failures are yours to claim as the leader.

Taking Credit for What They Do

1-2-12. Now that you have learned the importance of surrounding yourself with people that are smarter than you, it's time to "take credit for what they do." You're the organization or team leader. The success of your team in accomplishing their mission, task, or goal is your responsibility. When they succeed, it's your success. Claim it and own it. It's not about arrogance or pride; it's your job. When your team is successful, there will be all sorts of people who will claim responsibility for that success. Your team members will waste little time breaking their arms patting themselves on the back for their pivotal role in the team's achievements. As the leader you need to keep this in check. The win is yours; likewise the loss is yours as well.

1-2-13. If your team fails, misses the mark, or doesn't achieve the goals set for you, it is highly unlikely that anyone on your team will rush to claim responsibility. They may seek out praise for success, but they will flee from criticism. As the leader, it's your job to take the responsibility for your team's failure. In the unlikely scenario where you have a team member who wants to claim responsibility for the team's failure, you must keep them in check as well. You don't get to take credit for what your team does unless you take credit for *everything* that they do. Win or lose, it's *your* responsibility as the leader. That's really what it means to "take credit for what they do."

Taking Credit for Failure

1-2-14. Learning to claim both the success and the short-comings of your team is vital. We will start with your team's shortcomings and, at times, obvious failure. The reason to start with your team's shortcomings is because it is much easier to take credit for their successes than for their failures.

1-2-15. No leader or team is perfect. If you happen to be working for a leader or boss that thinks you should be perfect, find a new organization, because you will be unhappy following such lead-ership. Also, don't be that kind of leader. Taking responsibility for your organization's employees' or team's shortcomings will create an extreme amount of trust and cooperation. (There is more on trust and cooperation in Section Three). If you are quick to lay blame on someone on your team for failure, then your team will not trust you, and nor should they. They will not support your decisions and may even undermine your oppor-tunity for success. Nor do you allow someone to take the fall for you. If you are leading, you are responsible for any individual's failure. If you are calling the shots, making decisions, and approving of your team's direction toward accomplishing the goals set for you by the leadership above you, then the end results are yours to claim, whether good or bad.

1-2-16. *"Bad news does not get better with time!"* As a leader, this saying has been more than just words for me; it has been part of my leadership philosophy. You need to learn it and start employing it today as a leadership and life skill. Failure *seldom* comes as a surprise. Why as a team leader would you allow your team's failure or shortcomings to be a *surprise* to the leadership above you? If you wait for them to discover that something is not going as planned, then the next statement becomes even truer: "The s**t is going to hit the fan." You should *know* when things are not going according to plan. It's bound to happen at some point, and your job as the leader is to protect your team from the inevitable backlash that will come from the leadership above. As soon as you know that things are not going as planned, claim responsibility and demonstrate that you are working on solutions. Seek assistance and support. Asking for help is not a sign of weakness; in a young leader, it is a sign of brilliance. Protect your team, and they will work even harder for you.

1-2-17. There are times when projects or circumstances can change rapidly, and someone on your team can make a huge mistake without your knowledge. This is when you really step up and take responsibility as a leader. *Everyone* makes mistakes, and the extraordinary leader claims *all* the mistakes made by their team. Everyone will respect you for this style of leadership. You can deal with the individual or the circumstances causing problems later, but for now, it's all about *you* stepping up and taking command of your team.

Taking Credit for Success

1-2-18. Now it's time to take credit for your organization's and team's success. This is the easy part of being a leader. You should be proud of your leadership success. You should stand in front of the team and accept the rewards, the bonuses, the trophy, and the pats on the back for a job well done. You are the leader. It's not about being arrogant; it's your job.

1-2-19. Think about how this plays out anytime a sports team wins a championship. In professional sports, it's the team owner and general manager who accept the championship trophy, not the players. They are the team's top leadership. It's their job to put a team together and manage all the assets necessary to create a team that has the ability to win a championship. They receive the trophy first and get to make the first congratulatory speeches about how hard everyone has worked, how everyone has come together to make the championship possible, how they couldn't be more proud of their coaches and players. They talk about all the years they have put into building a champion-ship team. Then what happens? Pay close attention to this....

1-2-20. The team owner passes the trophy to the team's head coach. The head coach then thanks his players and other coaches for all the hard work they have put into becoming champions. Then the head coach passes the trophy to the team's overall most valuable player, who makes a speech about how they couldn't have done it without their team members. Then the team's overall most valuable player passes the trophy to the championship game's most valuable player, who makes a speech about how they couldn't have done it without the support of their team and the fans at the game.

1-2-21. Do you see what's happening here? It's not an accident that this same scenario plays out in every sport at every championship ceremony. It is the *leadership* that is responsible for the success of the team. It doesn't matter that neither the owner nor the general manager scored a single point. What matters is that they are the organization's leaders and it is their job to make everyone else successful.

1-2-22. The military does something very similar when it comes to awarding medals. Let's say there is a combat operation with 50 individual team members. The mission is accomplished and everyone returns. Although some have been wounded, everyone will survive. Every team member performed his or her job just as they had been trained. The operation wasn't perfect, of course, but the leadership adapted, improvised and overcame all obstacles. Also, they couldn't have done this mission without a huge amount of support from other units. By all measures the operation was a huge success.

1-2-23. So the top commanders decide this mission deserves special recognition. Award citations are filled out with input from those leading the mission, and a ceremony is planned. The highest award is issued to the command leader of the mission. Then special awards are issued to a few individuals who distinguished themselves in action, and to anyone who was injured (Purple Heart). Then the rest of the team is awarded a lower level award. You might think this isn't fair. Shouldn't everyone get the highest award since they all took the same risk?

No, not necessarily. The leader of the operation was ultimately responsible for its success and is awarded accordingly. And the command does reserve the right to issue special awards to individuals, as I mentioned. If the mission had been a failure, the operations command leader would have taken responsibility and been held accountable for its failure, not the entire team.

1-2-24. Don't miss what the leadership is doing in both the sports example and the military example. The leadership is not just accepting credit for the success of their team; they are then sharing the rewards of that success with their team.

Sharing the Reward

1-2-25. The only time that accepting credit for your organization and team success is *arrogant*, is when you fail to *share* the credit appropriately. There is no limit to the amount of good that you can do as long as you share the credit around. If, as the team leader, you are influencing your team correctly, everyone will work hard to accomplish the mission, tasks or goal. Your leadership should ensure that your teammates can accomplish what they would not be able to accomplish alone. Everyone deserves recognition for their efforts. It's your job to provide appropriate feedback, and acknowledgement, and reward, for your team's accomplishments. Don't take your team's work for granted, even if they are only doing their 'job.' Everyone needs encouragement. Take time to give your teammates the proper accolades and respect that they deserve. Be generous and genuine in your praise and you will build loyalty and trust.

For more on the power of praise, see part two, section two: Morale.

Section Three

Commitment

1-3-1. When I joined the Army, I swore an oath to uphold the constitution of the United States, to defend our nation, and to follow the orders of those appointed above me. Every soldier who joins the military takes an oath of service that signifies their individual commitment. Each soldier's commitment to serve has a different length based upon the type and complexity of training the military is going to be giving them. This is a two-way commitment. The military is committing to train an individual in a vast number of skills, and the individual is committing to complete their training and then serve a specific amount of time in return. Once your initial commitment is over, you may continue by reenlisting, or you may say thank you very much and depart the military for other opportunities. The military may also make the decision to terminate you at the end of your current commitment.

1-3-2. One question that I'm often asked is: "So when you join the Army, can you just decide to quit or leave anytime you want?" No, you cannot. You cannot just decide to quit one day. You are legally bound to fulfill your commitment. Imagine what would happen if this wasn't the case. The military has to know that each mission critical job is filled with a fully trained and qualified soldier. The government spends a significant amount of money making sure that each soldier is highly qualified for their individual job, and in return they expect you to stay around and do that job. If we train you to be a mechanic, medic, pilot, nurse, or infantry soldier, we are going to expect that you return a certain amount of your time for that training. 1-3-3. There are civilian jobs and companies that do the same thing. A good example is teachers and doctors. There are a lot of scholarships in both of these career fields that will pay for your schooling and training. When you are done, you are required to give your time and talents back to the communities that have helped fund your education. Most of the time, this means you are working in under-served communities that desperately need teachers and doctors. Another good example is welders. There are companies that will teach you to be a welder, but you have to commit to staying with the company for a specific amount of time in order to receive that training. If you later decide to leave before that time is up, you most often are required to pay the company for the training you received. This is true for doctors and teachers as well.

1-3-4. I'm a fan of requiring commitment, because there are a lot of advantages to this method of shared commitment, especially for the leader. If everyone on your team or in your department was required to sign a letter of commitment, how much easier would your job as the leader be? However, most leaders will not have this advantage when it comes to leading their team of employees. The people you will be leading will have the ability to walk out on you at any time, and that's a sucky feeling. One of the best ways to tell how effective you are at creating commitment among your team members is to look at the turnover rate. If the turnover rate is high, you might not be doing a great job as the leader. There is a saying: "people don't leave jobs; they leave bosses," and the reason for this statement is that most people when they leave a job take another job that is virtually identical to the one they left, and generally at the same pay rate. That being the case, you have to assume they are leaving the leadership, not the job.

1-3-5. How then do you build commitment among those whom you are leading? What do you have to *do* to make sure your team, organization or employees want to commit to you long-term? How do you create loyalty? The answer is simple, but implementing the answer can be difficult. The answer is: you have to build trust and cooperation. The research group Gallup, in their State of the American Work Place Survey, tells us that close to 80% of people are *not* motivated to do outstanding work because they do *not* feel that their leadership clearly communicates expectations and desired outcomes. And they do *not* feel that their leadership is demonstrating trust and cooperation within the organization. Trust and cooperation are built when you create a working environment that makes sure your team is informed, supplied, and encouraged; and when you do, they feel safe. When you're in an environment where you feel safe, you are more likely to produce outstanding work, and more likely to stay committed and loyal to the leadership.

Leaders Eat Last

Recently, bestselling author, motivational speaker and Internet star Simon Sinek wrote the book *Leaders Eat Last: Why Some Teams Pull Together and Others Don't*. It's an excellent book and I recommend that you place it on your list of leadership books to read.

That being said, what Sinek refers to in *Leaders Eat Last* is an age old military tradition. As the leader, you literally eat last. Why? Eating last builds trust and cooperation. It demonstrates to your troops, or to your organization's team, that they matter, that you are willing to put them first, that *their* needs come before anything else. It makes them feel valued and safe; and when you feel safe inside your organization, you are more likely to help protect the organization and the team that is making you feel safe.

Why do soldiers, both men and woman, put themselves in harm's way to accomplish dangerous missions, ones that could easily take their lives? What drives them? Are soldiers somehow braver than the average person, or are they indoctrinated in such a way that they only act without thought? Neither is true. Soldiers have a universal answer for why we do what we do: "...because my buddies would do it for me." It's the ultimate act of trust and cooperation.—*Illustration 5*

1-3-6. We all commit to groups and organizations and leadership because we believe in what they do, or because we gain something from being part of that group, including gaining our income. We want to be part of something we can be proud of, or that makes us feel we're making a difference in some way.

Ways to Build Commitment as a Leader

1-3-7. As a leader you can easily stand out by implementing the following elements in your organization.

a) Lead by example. If you are not demonstrating commitment in your actions, why would you expect anyone else to be committed?

b) Employ good communication skills. Make sure that your team is informed, and that they feel you have listened to their input and valued their input.

c) Have you ever tried to build or repair something without the right tools? It creates a level of frustration that makes you want to quit. Make sure your team has the proper tools to do their jobs well.

d) Define the expectations you have for your team members upfront. Make sure you communicate what you expect of them regarding their time, their abilities and their standard of work. This is vitally important when you're working with volunteers. Leading volunteers is a tricky business. They are working and participating for free on their own time, and they can leave you at any moment. Building trust and cooperation with your volunteers is a must if you plan on keeping them over time.

e) Set high standards. People want to be part of organizations that produce a quality product or result. So set high standards and hold yourself and the organization accountable to those standards.

f) Accomplish something big, something that makes a difference to others. People want to be part of something that is making a difference. Do this even if it means doing it outside of the "normal parameters" of work. Maybe you're leading an organization that makes widgets. Widgets are important, but maybe there are people who cannot afford your widgets in a war devastated country. Find a way to give some of those widgets away. Your team will be proud of making widgets, I promise.

g) Find ways to continue your team's education and training. This creates personal self-esteem and shows them you value their progress.

h) Make sure everyone has something to do. This might sound strange, but too often people are actually idle and feel like they are not doing anything important. This can be especially true when dealing with volunteers. It's better to tell someone you don't need their help than to let someone volunteer and then not have anything significant for them to do.

i) Support the leaders above you. I've seen too often how young leaders can lose their team members by being poor team members themselves. You can't trash the leaders above you and expect your team to believe you will not do the same to them.

The Results of a Committed Team

1-3-8. When you create an environment of trust and cooperation, your team will be committed. They will produce outstanding results because they are proud of what they are doing and for whom they are doing it. Committed teams create momentum, and momentum means you are progressing toward your stated goals. People are attracted to teams that are obviously working together, and teams that are producing quality results and products. Commitment is what keeps teams and organizations together when things get difficult, and things always get difficult. If team members are committed, they will rally around each other and support the process, hold true to the vision you've created, and make sure everyone is safe.

The 40% Rule

The 40% rule is attributed to the Navy Seals; however, I heard the same 40% rule used throughout my Army training as well. The rule applies when you believe that you are completely physically and mentally exhausted. You know deep down that you have nothing else left to give. You believe you have given your all, and that you are 100% done. But in reality, you are only 40% done. You still have 60% more to give.

I don't believe that anyone can give more than 100% of themselves to something; 100% is all that anyone can offer. However, I do believe in the 40% rule. The 40% rule is backed by a number of scientific studies. In order to give 100% physically and mentally, you are actually pushing your body past its ability to function; your body's vital systems are shutting down as you reach the 100% level.

An example of 100% physical and mental commitment can be seen during the Ironman Triathlon. I'm sure most of us have seen images of these athletes collapsing along the grueling course, some well before the finish line, others only steps away, and still others as they cross the finish. Still, many of the top athletes finish and sometimes it seems as if they could just keep on going. Perhaps they could?

The key to applying the 40% rule is perseverance, grit, and most of all, having other committed team members at your side. I can tell you that there were a number of times in my military training when I was totally ready to quit—to do the unthinkable and DOR (drop on request), but I always had someone alongside me who would not allow me to give up. In turn, I was at times the person who would not allow my buddies to give up. In the military, you are never alone. There is always someone there to help you push beyond your 40% and move you closer to 100%. There is also always someone there to catch you if you have reached your 100%.—*Illustration 6*

Section Four

Time Management

1-4-1. As a young Second Lieutenant on my first assignment, I was totally overwhelmed with the amount of work I had to accomplish on a daily basis. Adding to the actual work I had to get done was my desire to be the first to arrive and the last to leave (see Illustration 3). This meant I was arriving at the office at 4:45 a.m. six days a week, and not leaving most nights until 7:00 p.m. I was killing myself. I was totally exhausted within six months, and burnout was close behind. Fortunately, about that time I had begun to master some vital time management skills. I was still the first to arrive and the last to leave, but I was able to accomplish more each day, all while significantly reducing my stress level. I started to enjoy my job and take on new challenges. Then I was given full command of that unit, which was unusual for my experience and rank.

1-4-2. As a young leader, you are going to have a number of new responsibilities, and also schedules to keep. You have to exercise self-discipline when it comes to your time. Time is a limited resource and it is always running out. You cannot stop it, slow it down, or get any wasted time back. Time management skills will increase your productivity, allow for flexibility, and reduce stress.

1-4-3. Many students are fond of boasting about how great they are at multi-tasking. Some even pride themselves on *how many* things they believe they can do all at the same time. The problem with this thinking is that it is *wrong*. You are not functioning as some kind of highly efficient multi-tasker getting all kinds of things done at once. The reality is you are not accomplishing any of the tasks that you are multi-tasking at in a very effective manner. Multi-tasking is a *myth*. You cannot multi-task. Science says it's not possible, and I'm telling you now.

1-4-4. I may have just hurt your feelings. Your pride may be injured by learning that multi-tasking is a myth. You may even disagree with me, but the latest neuroscience is on my side. Dr. John Medina, in his New York Times bestselling book *Brain Rules*, provides scientific evidence that what you are actually doing is "task switching." Yes, you can switch from one task to another rapidly, but that does not mean you are multi-tasking. Neuroscience tells us that there is a start and stop going on between tasks. What your brain is doing is switching back and forth rapidly, because your brain can do only one thing at a time. Every time your brain stops doing one task, it has to restart in order to do the next task. The result of your "multi-tasking" is that you are not giving your best to *any* of the tasks you are working on. Your productivity is suffering.

1-4-5. So when you're listening to music and reading, you're not actually doing both at the same time. If you're texting while in a meeting, you're not paying attention to the meeting; you're texting. Stop right now and develop the self-discipline needed to focus on what you should be doing at any given moment, and you will become more productive.

1-4-6. One of the best and first steps you as a leader need to take in order to have good time management skills is to learn to set goals for yourself and your team. Goals should outline the work that needs to be accomplished and state the timeframe in which it needs to be completed. Leadership is all about influencing others to get stuff done. You're the leader, so you set the goals and then focus the team's attention on accomplishing those goals.

Are You Wasting Time or Saving Time?

1-4-7. Attempt to find where time is being wasted in your day. Where can you save time? Here is a list of some classic time wasters and time savers.

Time Wasters:

a) Failure to start. Young leaders are especially susceptible to this time waster. You spend way too much time getting ready to get stuff done and then you never actually get anything done. Sometimes you have to start with what you know and what you have. Maybe you're missing a team member you'd like to have, but that doesn't need to stop the rest of the team from working toward the goals. You can adjust as you go along, but get started.

b) Worry. You are feeling unsure, so you waste time looking busy and not really doing anything. Most of the time you can solve this dilemma by asking for help. Remember that asking for help is not a sign of weakness; it's a sign of brilliance.

c) Checking your email every five minutes. You are wasting time. Learn to manage your email inbox so it doesn't manage *you*. When I was young, it wasn't an email inbox; it was an actual basket on my desk for physical mail. This inbox could fill up several times each day. Now it's an email inbox that can become overwhelming. I used to say: "I only open mail when I have time to deal with it right then." Then I learned to do the same thing when it became email; I only opened my email when I had time to deal with what was there on the spot. There are people who get hundreds of emails a day, and they stop what they are doing every time they get a new one. You have to manage your emails before they take over your productivity. There are a lot of techniques for dealing with email; I would encourage you to find one that works for you and stick to it.

d) No "open door policy." I often hear leaders say: "My door is always open." If it is, you are never going to get anything done. You cannot stop what you are doing every time someone wants to discuss something, ask a question, or chat. Your physical door or metaphorical door should never be open all the time. You should be accessible to your team, but set times on your calendar when they can make appointments. Then schedule time when you can check in with them as well. Keep open lines of communication but not an open door.

e) Social media can be a productivity killer, especially when it is your personal social media taking your time at work. Be careful; this could cost you your position. Social media can have some significant advantages for you and your team, but it has to be carefully managed.

f) Don't procrastinate. Get it done now and deal with it only once. If you start something, finish it.

g) Don't let meetings be an alternative to work. Meetings are essential for lots of reasons, but too often we have meetings that accomplish nothing. Don't let others control your productivity with time-stealing meetings.

h) Leaders are delegators. So delegate jobs to your team. Make sure they understand the mission, tasks, and goals, and then give your team the resources they need and let them do their jobs. You are a leader, so lead; don't micromanage your team members. You have your own work to do.

Time Savers:

a) Use a calendar to set up your schedule, make appointments, make to-do lists, and set priorities for yourself and your team.

b) Get organized and clear up the clutter. You don't have to be a neat freak or hyper organized, but piles of crap lying around are a sure sign you are not working efficiently. Our email inbox is often where we hide our clutter. No one knows it's there but it's there nonetheless. Always have a work email and a personal email to help cut down on your work email clutter.

c) Schedule meetings for your team. I know I warned you that meetings are time wasters. However, some meetings are essential. The key to effective meetings is setting a prioritized agenda and a time limit. Some meetings may need to be long, but most do not. With a prioritized agenda and a time limit, you are more productive. If you don't get to an item on the agenda, you can often deal with it at the next meeting.

d) Do not put unneeded effort into projects. Know when

the goals have been met and move on. There are times that will call for perfection, but in most cases there comes a time when additional effort doesn't yield additional results.

e) Learn to say no. Sometimes the best answer you can offer is 'no.' Leaders have a tendency to overextend their ability to get stuff done. You probably know the saying: "If you want something done, give it to a busy person." This saying comes from the fact that productive leaders have good time management skills and simply get more done then others do. But you have to ask yourself if what is being asked of you fits the current mission, tasks, and goals that have been set. If the answer is "they do not," then learn to say no.

1-4-8. Managing your time is an essential leadership skill, and time is truly a limited resource. Today's highly technological workplace can create a great deal of time wasting opportunities as well as time saving opportunities. Use your workplace technology to your benefit, and be careful not to allow it to become a distraction. As the leader, set the standard when it comes to time management, stay focused, and help your team to stay focused.

Part One Summary

1-4-9. I'd like to reemphasize that the military model of leadership is a superior training method. It has historically provided young individuals with the opportunity to lead others at younger ages than any other leadership model. Army leadership starts by teaching you the basic foundations of leadership and then quickly advances you to take command of yourself so that you can command others.

1-4-10. We have now covered some very important next-level leadership skills: self-leadership, developing a team, what it takes to create and maintain commitment within your team, and the importance of time management. Now it's time to march onward to even more advanced leadership skills. These skills are more complicated and will take you longer to develop. They are the leadership skills that, when mastered, will set you apart not only from your peers but also from 'average' leaders beyond your age.

Part Two

Marching Onward

Section One

Communication

2-1-1. Since being the leader is about influencing others to get stuff done, you have to actually get them to *do* stuff. Hopefully, they are going to accomplish what you have clearly defined for them as the mission, task, or goal. How do you do this? It's called communication. As a leader, being able to clearly communicate your intent to your team is an absolute *must*. I'd like to emphasize again that communication is a *leadership skill* that can be learned, practiced and eventually mastered.

2-1-2. Communication is about transmitting information so that it is clearly understood by all members of your organization and teams. After all, if your people can't understand what you're asking them to do, their failure is certain. If people don't understand you, they will not be engaged and cannot follow you!

The Military Operations Order (OPORD)

When you are an Army officer, military communication comes in the form of a seemingly simple 5-paragraph operations order or OPORD. These paragraphs consist of 1) Situation 2) Mission 3) Execution 4) Sustainment and 5) Command and Control. Each of these paragraphs has multiple subparagraphs which you are expected to know. The OPORD is considered a living, breathing form of communication that requires flexibility in changing circumstances. It requires written and verbal leadership skills to complete and execute. The vital information within any OPORD will eventually be filtered down to the newest private in the unit. The most important OPORD element for every soldier is to understand the Commander's *intent*. The Commander's intent describes what constitutes success for the operation. It includes the operation's purpose and the conditions that define the end state, or what the desired outcome will be.

Leaders fail when they don't communicate their intent or their end state. You don't have to be leading a military unit to appreciate the need for your team, volunteers, or employees to have a clear understanding of what you're trying to accomplish, why you're doing it the way you are, and what defines success.

When Gallup released its 2016 *State of the American Workplace* survey, one of the most revealing findings was that only 21% of employees agreed that they were led in a way that motivated them to do outstanding work! So why are the vast majority of employees not motivated to do outstanding work? Because leadership is not clearly communicating their expectations and desired outcomes, their employees don't understand the leadership's intent.

Corporations are tripping over themselves trying to understand and figure out how to implement the OPORD philosophy within their organizations. In order to succeed, young leaders need to be aware of this essential tool.—*Illustration 7*

2-1-3. As a leader in today's society, you will have to master not only written communication, verbal communication, and the art of active listening (receiving information), but also social media communication. That's right, social media is now a vital form of communication that is part of your leader's toolbox.

2-1-4. As a young officer, I learned that there are two basic forms of communication: one-way and two-way. These are horizontal forms of communicating. The commander would issue an order or directive to the troops below them so they could accomplish a mission. Then one of two things would happen.

2-1-5. In one-way communication there was no opportunity for input. Your input was not asked for or welcomed. You were expected to accomplish the mission as directed—period. This form of communication is most often associated with an authoritative style of leader. The leader makes the decisions, gives the orders, and you follow them. Of course, this style is not reserved for military leaders. As a matter of fact, I've seen more people in the civilian world that operate in this manner than do military commanders.

2-1-6. Then there was two-way communication. Two-way communication allowed for the commander's subordinates to collect information, ask questions, and offer input. In two-way communication, the commander would provide additional information, answer questions, listen to and receive input, and then make a decision. Once the decision was made, it was your job to accomplish it.

2-1-7. All this might sound harsh, but it is a highly effective way of getting large groups of people and equipment on task quickly. However, in today's Army, things have changed in the way we communicate. So let's establish a base line as we move forward.

Leadership Communication Skills

Written Communication

2-1-8. As a leader you have to be able to communicate your intent clearly in writing. Generally speaking, email is now our number one form of written communication, and it has made us lazy and complacent. Email is great for communicating factual information, but don't assume in a short, quick email that you have communicated any level of passion, desire, humor or even displeasure. University professors consistently complain that students arrive at their universities without the ability to communicate in written form.

What's the Big Deal Anyway?

I was teaching my intermediate and advanced leadership training skills workshop for a group of high school students. Then one student said; "What's the big deal about written communication anyway? Nobody really reads any more. The only books I've read in the last two years were for school, and I can't honestly tell you that I actually read all of those. Everything I read is in some form of Internet shorthand."

To some extent he was right. Studies tell us that the majority of people have not read one complete book in the past year. But those in the majority are also not your average leader. I find this is remarkably sad, and also very telling. According to Darren Hardy of *Success Magazine*, *every* highly successful leader, in *every* career field, is an avid reader. That should tell you a great deal about your own ability to lead, and it points us back to our earlier topic of self-discipline.

• • •

As a person with dyslexia, I have a great deal of trouble when it comes to grammar, sentence structure, and spelling. I'm the king of the run-on sentence and the comma splice, and I can't spell to save my life. Yet, my content is typically considered to be better than most. My dyslexia is certainly a problem when it comes to written communication, but it's a weakness that I have learned to manage. I surround myself with team members who can edit my writing so I can clearly communicate in written form to my subordinates, my team members, and especially to those readers who have helped me become a bestselling author by purchasing my books.—*Illustration 8*

2-1-9. Here is what I can guarantee: if you want to be an exceptional leader you will have to be able to communicate clearly in writing. The internet is not going to reduce written communication to some form of email shorthand. You need to hone your writing skills. If you're like me, you will need to find people who can help you manage this area of weakness.

Verbal Communication

2-1-10. It's been said that people fear speaking in public more than they fear death. I've never found a study that accurately confirms this statement, but we can be sure that most people would rather not stand up in front of a group of people and speak. And for most people this is particularly unappealing if they are asked to speak in front of a group of their peers. But speaking in public is a skill that can be learned, invested in, and even mastered if you are willing. Not every leader needs to be a public speaker but you have to be able to communicate verbally.

2-1-11. Every leadership position is going to require you to communicate orally with your team. It's vital that you can clearly articulate the mission, tasks and goals you are asking your team to accomplish. Have you ever been on a team with someone who just can't seem to get their point across verbally? You may even have heard them say something like: "Just do what I meant, not what I said." This is a failure to communicate, and it's not oaky. Your subordinates are not mind readers, no matter how much you wish they were. Working under a leader that can't communicate verbally what they need their team to accomplish is one of the most frustrating things to deal with if you are a team member.

2-1-12. If this is an area of weakness for you, seek out opportunities to gain more experience. Don't live in fear. If you're shy, that's okay; volunteer to give a presentation to your team members or organization. Your peers actually *want* to see you succeed. Believe it or not, they are actually on your side, and they want you to be on *their* side. When you're in a meeting or communicating with your team, ask them what they heard you say. Their responses will confirm that you have actually *communicated* your intent and then everyone will be on the same page. This is a technique that every leader should use to make sure they have properly communicated with their team.

Active Listening

2-1-13. This is an area where many individuals and many leaders get themselves in trouble. Haven't we all sat with someone we are trying to talk with, only to have them completely ignore or not acknowledge what we're saying? Maybe you're talking to someone and they are on their phone checking whatever it is they might be checking. Or perhaps it's their body language that is sending you a clear message that they are not listening or that they are in total disagreement with what you are saying, but they aren't saying anything. Maybe you have said, "We need to talk," only to be given a dismissive wave and told, "Okay, we'll talk later." We have all been there, and most of us have been on both sides of this listening dilemma.

2-1-14. As a leader you need to learn to become an *active listener*. Active listening is just what it sounds like. You are actively listening to what someone is saying. You are fully concentrating on the message that someone else is sharing with you. You are not just passively *hearing* them talk. Active listening is when you are giving someone your full and undivided attention.

2-1-15. Becoming an active listener is not very difficult. Leaders that communicate active listening skills to their team build trust and cooperation with their team. Trust and cooperation is foundational to creating a working environment that helps people feel valued and increases their engagement. Even though you are the leader, your team doesn't always have to agree with your decisions, and it's unlikely they will agree with you all the time. However, if they believe that you have actually listened and heard what they have said, and seriously considered their opinions, they will feel validated. This validation builds rapport, and this rapport allows your team to work in an atmosphere of trust and cooperation. When there is trust and cooperation, your team will be much more likely to support you and the decisions you make.

Non-verbal Communication

2-1-16. Non-verbal communication is all about what you are and are not saying with your physical presence. It amuses me to watch students and see how much they don't understand about communicating non-verbally. Active listening is a great example because it is really all about non-verbal communication.

2-1-17. Active listening requires you as the leader to first stop what you are doing and give the person who is speaking your full and undivided attention. The person speaking to you needs to *see* you listening to them. It's your job to make eye contact with them, and to stand or sit in such a way that communicates you are involved in the conversation. Lean into the person speaking without invading their personal space. The speaker expects some sort of affirmation from you physically, so nod your head, for example, and be aware of your body language. You also need to understand negative body language. Don't stare at people. Don't cross your arms, or, when sitting, lean away from the person speaking to you. These are physical behaviors that send signals that you're not listening or that you're in disagreement with them (even if you are not). Just giving someone a "thumbs up" sign can give them the confidence that they have been heard.

2-1-18. There are many scientific studies that have been conducted to determine how much we actually communicate nonverbally. One of the most quoted studies was conducted by Dr. Albert Mehrabian, author of *Silent Messages*. His findings were shocking. The results showed that 93% of what we communicate to others is nonverbal. There are other studies suggesting that Mehrabian's figure is high, but what is abundantly clear in all the studies is that **most of what we communicate to others is nonverbal**.

2-1-19. Nonverbal communication is so important that I want to encourage you to study the subject in more detail. This book is not the place for a detailed discussion of nonverbal communication, but what I will do is highlight a few areas to get you thinking about how you communicate nonverbally.

   a) Posture: The Army refers to this as 'military bearing.' It's about how you carry yourself and how you stand. Are your shoulders back? Is your head up? Do you have your hands in your pockets? (Never put your hand in your pocket when in uniform). Pay attention to your movements: Are you crossing your arms over your chest when someone is speaking to you? How you sit and what you do with your legs send all sorts of positive or negative signals.

b) Eye contact: People feel engaged with you when you make eye contact with them. Good eye contact conveys trust and trustworthiness. However, there is a fine line between good eye contact and staring.

c) Touch: Touch is a powerful form of nonverbal communication. My experience working with student leadership organizations clearly tells me that students are taught to offer a firm handshake upon meeting someone new. That's because a firm handshake communicates confidence and a sense of welcome to the other person. Appropriate touch can be very powerful and yet tricky to learn. You don't want to cross into someone's personal space, as this will definitely impede your ability to influence people and ultimately your leadership ability.

Training Service Dogs and
Nonverbal Communication

Several years ago I started volunteering with an organization that trains service dogs.* I was excited about this opportunity because of the fantastic work the organization does with veterans, children with Autism, and other individuals in need. My training started out with being a weekend pup-sitter and then fostering dogs in training. I quickly progressed through the program and earned my certification as a volunteer trainer with public access. This simply meant I could take the dogs out in public for training purposes. What does this have to do with nonverbal communication? It has *everything* to do with it.

I had trained soldiers for combat and spent years in the classroom with junior high students, so surely I was qualified to train a dog. But I was *wrong!* There is nothing ordinary about what we are asking these dogs to do, and nor is the training for the dog or the handler ordinary.

Dogs don't speak English. Really? I'd always assumed that dogs spoke English as their native language. It turns out that I don't speak dog either. Dogs and humans communicate almost exclusively in nonverbal ways. This was a huge lesson for me about how much I was unintentionally communicating nonverbally. Training with these dogs reminded me so much about my body posture, the tone of my voice, and how important it is to stay calm because the dogs pick up your personal vibe. One big lesson was how much you communicate to the dog by the way you handle the leash.

My training with these very special dogs was such a powerful reminder of my need to hone my personal nonverbal skills. If you'd like more information on the organization I'm speaking about, please look them up: Palmetto Animal Assisted Life Services (PAALS) in Columbia, South Carolina. www.paals.org.

—*Illustration 9*

Social Media Communication

2-1-20. A generally accepted definition of social media is: a group of internet web and mobile based technologies that allow individuals to create and exchange *user generated* content. The user based content is shared on many different media communication platforms, including websites, blogs, chat rooms, forums, websites, video platforms, podcasts, and social dialogue networks (Facebook, LinkedIn, Twitter, Pinterest, Instagram, Snapchat, YouTube, Vimeo, and others).

2-1-21. Social media is a widely used and *powerful* communication tool. As a leader you will have to learn to navigate the ever-changing social media landscape. Many of these platforms are here today and gone tomorrow, which makes your job even more difficult. You may not have heard of the onetime rising social media star Myspace. Myspace was all the rage in the late 1990's, but Myspace lost out quickly to Facebook. You may be more familiar with Vine Video's or Periscope's live video formats; both became fast growing social media video platforms that gained popularity quickly and then virtually disappeared overnight. One currently very popular platform is Snapchat. Social media experts are debating Snapchat's ability to survive against other platforms that are offering similar features with greater technological backing, App integration, and support. If the experts are right, Snapchat will be a social media platform of the past. What does all this mean for you as a leader and what questions are you facing? What will the next generation of social media look like, and how will you as a leader deal with the changes?

2-1-22. Let's take a quick look at some data from the current social media platforms, according to Pew Research: 69% of all

Americans are on some form of social media, and that number is only expected to increase; 90% of all individuals age 18-29 use one or more forms of social media. The most widely used platforms in order of use are: Facebook, Pinterest, Instagram, LinkedIn, and Twitter. If the current trend holds, Instagram is the new rising star expected to overtake Pinterest. It's important to note that the vast majority of individuals use some form of social media *daily*.

2-1-23. Social media is now part of our everyday lives. This includes being part of our daily *working* lives, and thus, you'll need to be a social media leader. Sources such as Gallup, Pew Research, Forbes, and Success Magazine are all telling us that employees expect their leadership to be using and leading the way on social media. This provides you, as a young leader, with a great deal of opportunity as well as challenges. Let's take a closer look at the challenges and advantages of being a social media leader.

Being a Social Media Leader
2-1-24. *Challenges:*

a) Social media is *public media*. Everything you post is available for use by others. Don't be fooled by so called "disappearing media." There is always a trail or signature left from everything you post. As a leader, it's your job to set the standard in the use of social media. Your team or tribe will follow your lead in subject matter and the tone that you use on social media.

b) Dealing with multiple social media platforms can be difficult with so many platforms available to you and your team. If upper management has set a standard for which platforms the organization will be using, then your job is a little easier. Stick with the plan of the organization. If no plan is in place, it's best for you, as the leader, to select no more than two of those platforms and stick to them as your primary social media. If your organization is using more than two platforms, make a personal choice as to which two best suit your team's needs and stay focused on them. Make sure that the individuals that you answer to also know your social media plans.

c) Messaging platforms are the newest form of social media, and the sheer number of these can be challenging as well. If you and your team use a messaging platform to communicate, make sure that the leadership above you is included in the platform and your communication loops. Never create a "secret" group or messaging loop that your boss does not know about. It will get you in a huge amount of trouble.

d) Social media creates a new form of "transparency" for everyone in the organization. But transparency can create a sense of familiarity that can blur the lines between leadership and team membership. Be careful to maintain appropriate relationships.

e) It's best to create a social media policy. The policy should set the guidelines for everyone as to what is appropriate to post on social media. If your organization uses open social media platforms such as Facebook and Instagram, you will need to make sure everyone understands what is appropriate to post on these sites.

f) Monitoring your social media platforms can be extremely challenging. This is a good reason to keep the number of platforms you use down to just two. As the organizational leader, you have to set aside time to check your social media platforms daily. This can be a responsibility that is dedicated to a team member, but remember: if you're responsible for the content, you better be checking the sites regularly.

2-1-25. *Advantages:*

a) Social media is *fun.* It is a great way to create *esprit de corps*, build moral, and motivate your team and tribe. Even the Army has embraced the use of social media; soldiers in basic training are allowed to use their cell phone to take pictures and post different elements of their training on social media.

I have to confess, as an old time veteran soldier, that this trend makes me cringe. The fact that soldiers are allowed to keep their phones is shocking to me. Back in the day when I went to basic training, I was allowed two phone calls. My first call was to let my mom know I had arrived for training and was currently alive. The second call I was allowed to make was about five weeks into training to let my mom know I was still alive and that I would call her when I graduated. Both calls were collect calls. Do you even know what a collect call is?

b) Social media creates transparency. As a leader it allows you to communicate openly with your organization. You can share milestone successes and offer encouragement to everyone on the team. Often, different members of your team are disconnected from what other members are doing, and social media allows everyone an opportunity to stay connected.

c) Many younger members of your organization are less connected to email than older members. Younger members may not even check their email, if they even have an email, more than once every few days. There are times when, if you're working with younger members on your team, the most efficient way to communicate quickly with the team is through social media.

d) Social media is a great way to create a higher level of engagement throughout your organization. When everyone feels that they know what is going on in the organization, they feel greater connection to the organization and are more engaged in its success.

e) Social media can provide you with immediate feedback. It also allows you to *offer* immediate feedback. Your team will be quick to respond to you through social media, letting you know how things are going. A word of caution: don't use social media as a two-way communication tool between you and an individual. Not everyone needs to be in on the conversation between you and someone else.

f) Most everyone reading this book already belongs to, or is a member of, some student organization such as a CTSO, Student Council, Leadership Summit, 4-H, FFA, Greek Community, and many other student leadership organizations and clubs. This means that your organization has already created a social media following and platform on sites like Facebook, Twitter, LinkedIn, Instagram, and YouTube.

This means you can make use of the *most important advantage* of social media: **sharing your message**. You and your entire team can literally share your message to most of the world. You can promote your brand, products, events, successes, and your team members. You can show what you do and why you do it. You can sell products, raise money, and share the amazing opportunities that you offer to others. If used correctly, social media is one of the tools, if not the very best tool, that you have to recruit others to join you and your organization. Take advantage of the platform you already have.

2-1-26. One additional advantage I'd like to highlight is social media's ability to create a *specific* media platform. If you don't already have an organization that has a social media presence on the web, you can create one. The sky is the limit when it comes to your ability to be creative and grow a social media following reaching countless people. So if you have a message, product, video, idea, or cause that you want to share with the world, take advantage of the vast reach that social media has to offer.

Section Two

Morale: A Primary Leadership Function

2-2-1. Teaching young leaders about *morale* has taken a back-seat to virtually every leadership method or theory. We typically teach you leadership styles and motivational techniques, and fill your head with engagement statistics. And all the while we ignore the core principle of *morale*. Companies of all sizes have forgotten the importance of morale, and it's starting to show. As leaders we have shifted the focus off the *collective cohesiveness* of our organizations and onto the *individual*. We have placed so much emphasis on individuals that we are having trouble functioning as part of the larger organizational structure.

2-2-2. It's not always about *you*. As a leader you don't have time to make everyone happy, and happiness is a feeling you cannot control for other individuals. As a leader, it's your job to *influence* others. Sure, there will be times that you will be working one-on-one with team members, especially when you are new to your leadership position. But remember to focus your attention on the *collective* needs of the organization first, and how that ultimately benefits every individual. That is what morale is all about.

2-2-3. I'd like to define morale as: the collective capacity of a group of people to maintain confidence, cohesiveness, and discipline, and to trust in the organizational leadership's ability to build cooperation and to persevere in obtaining the goals that have been set.

Army Morale Defined

Morale is the human dimension's most important intangible element. It's a measure of how people feel about themselves, their team, and their leaders. High morale comes from good leadership, shared hardship, and mutual respect. It's an emotional bond that springs from common values like loyalty to fellow soldiers and a belief that the organization will care for families. High morale results in a cohesive team that enthusiastically strives to achieve common goals. Leaders know that morale is an essential human element that holds the team together and keeps the team going in the face of the terrifying and dispiriting things that occur in war.

—*Illustration 10*

2-2-4. Morale is an emotional state, and it is typically measured as being high or low. Morale is most often measured by how people in the organization generally feel about how things are going overall. Although morale is not something we can actually measure, we can collect information and data by surveying the organization's teams and employees. Morale is most often linked to productivity. So when productivity is high, morale is generally reported as being high as well. Strangely enough, however, productivity can be slipping while morale is still high because morale is about overall confidence, cohesiveness, and discipline. If the leadership is instilling these elements within their organization, morale can remain high in a production downturn.

2-2-5. In times of economic downturn, the first reaction of many companies is to see only the numbers and not the people. Fixing the numbers means trimming expenses. One of the greatest expenses of any company large or small is employee salaries. So companies lay off or fire employees to trim expenses, and morale drops as a direct result. People are afraid of losing their jobs. Think back to part one, section three, where we discussed commitment and the importance of trust and cooperation. Morale will fall if your team doesn't believe that you "have their back." Companies that find alternative ways (other than letting go of employees) to deal with times of economic downturn will keep morale high. The reason is simple: employees have a higher level of confidence that leadership will work to protect them.

2-2-6. Maintaining organizational success and morale is a tricky balancing act for leadership. The leadership above you expects results, and your team wants to be emotionally protected and invested in what they are doing. I believe that morale is best maintained as a top-down leadership function rather than a bottom-up leadership function. By that I mean: morale starts at the top of the leadership chain, not at the bottom. Yet as a young leader you are at the bottom of the leadership chain and need to maintain the morale of your team.

2-2-7. So how do you as a young leader build and maintain morale? As with most things in leadership, you have to set the example. Morale is an intangible emotional state that you have the ability to shape; it is determined by your attitude, your self-discipline, and your commitment to the team and organizational goals. You are frontline leadership. People are watching and listening for you to set the standard. If you trash how things are being done and how things are going, your team will follow in step, and that will not be productive. Take time to highlight the results your team is achieving and the fact that they are reaching their goals. Give your team reasons to want to achieve their goals and make a difference, and they will work for you and for the team. The choice is yours. It is your job to lead the march forward.

2-2-8. Here are some additional steps you can employ to *build and maintain* high morale.

    a) Make sure you have developed the right team for the job. "One bad apple spoils the whole bunch" is an accurate saying when it comes to organizational morale. Just one or two key players can destroy morale. As the leader, you have to keep your team working together, and sometimes that may mean removing from your team someone who is not a team player. Move with caution when you are considering removing someone from your team. A sense of morale is an emotional state, and you may find that with just a minor adjustment, your "bad apple" can make the necessary changes.

    b) Make sure your team is well trained to get the job done. Asking people to do something they are not trained or prepared to do is a sure morale killer. Frustration rises rapidly when team members are not well trained.

    c) Make sure you have the necessary supplies and staff. Leaders are being asked to do more with less all the time. However, everyone needs the basic tools, supplies and personnel to accomplish their jobs. Your budget has to support your mission.

    d) Don't forget about the physical space you are asking people to work in. This might sound silly but working environments have a significant impact on how people believe they are valued (see Illustration 11: Coke or Pepsi), and therefore how they work.

    A poorly functioning heating and cooling system,

broken office furniture, old computers and dated office equipment say a lot about how much value is placed upon personnel. The military is sometimes criticized for its seemingly obsessive need to upgrade and replace equipment. However, we all need to realize that equipment breaks and gets worn out while training. It does not always mean that it is obsolete, just old and broken, and there is nothing inexpensive about replacing equipment in the military or in civilian work factories and offices. If you've ever been asked to do work without the proper tools and equipment, you know how difficult it is to stay emotionally invested in your work and in your leadership.

e) Give your team the space to be creative, and invite initiative. Studies tell us that when we allow teams to have the time to be creative and apply initiative, they are more productive in all aspects of their work. Allow them to make appropriate decisions for their experience level; they don't have to do it your way to do it the right way.

f) Build excitement and enthusiasm. Keep your team informed of progress and award them accordingly. We all want to know we are doing a good job. As a leader, make sure you are communicating how well your team is progressing. Too often we tend to focus on the negative side of what we're doing.

h) Compensate your team appropriately. As a young leader, you may have little control of your team's salary and compensation packages; but that does not mean you cannot advocate for them. It also might mean that you can be creative in finding ways to compensate for a job well done. When it comes to maintaining high morale, people report that time off is more important than money. We sometimes 'work ourselves to death.' Find ways of rewarding your team's effort with the time factor. Allowing time for creativity in the workplace can be a reward, and of course time off is always a popular reward.

i) Be responsive when things do not go right. No one is perfect, including the leadership. This goes back to your role as an effective communicator. Be an active listener and respond fairly to each situation.

j) Take pride in what you do collectively. Morale is a collective emotion, and your team wants to be proud of what they are producing. They want to know that they are making a difference for themselves and their communities.

Coke or Pepsi

Shortly after taking a new position with a non-profit that provided work for adults with mental disabilities, I discovered there was a significant morale problem. My new team was functioning poorly, and there were a number of issues that I would, at some point, have to address.

I took a close look at what I could do in the shortest amount of time to positively affect morale. I noticed one thing on our workshop floor that was causing real issues: the two broken-down Coke machines. My staff said there was nothing we could do about them because we had a specific contract with Coke.

It only took a short time to figure out that we had an outdated contract with Coke. I contacted the local distributor and asked for new machines, and I was told it would be eight months to a year before we could get new machines. "No problem," I said.

I picked up the phone and called the regional Pepsi distributor. I told him the number of sodas we were going through in a month and asked if they would be interested in providing us with new machines. The distributor was more than happy to oblige, and he told me he would have two new high-volume machines delivered within two days. It was a done deal without a contract.

Next was my call back to the Coke distributorship, where I left a message for them to come and pick up their machines, because I had a new deal with Pepsi.

The Coke guy called right back: "What do you mean pick up the machines?"

I told him that I had a new deal with Pepsi and that I no longer needed or wanted his machines. He immediately wanted to know what he could do to assist me with my problem. I told him "Nothing, thank you; I have a new deal with Pepsi."

Two days later the Pepsi machines showed up.

You would have thought I had purchased a new car for everyone. When the Pepsi truck drove up, I had 150 people clapping and cheering. Morale is often about the little things.

Just as the Pepsi guy was leaving, the Coke distributor showed up with two new high-volume machines. He was too late, but after some negotiations I allowed him to leave one machine in another building, mostly because I drank Diet Coke.—*Illustration 11*

Morale versus Motivation

2-2-9. Do not confuse morale and motivation; they are not the same thing. Morale is a higher order function than motivation. Another way of saying this is that motivation is a byproduct of morale. Without positive morale, people lack motivation to succeed. Motivation is about personal desire rather than the *collective cohesiveness* of the organization. As a leader, it is easier to *motivate* than to build morale. You can "motivate someone," but you cannot "morale them."

2-2-10. Many of the things you do to build morale also help to build motivation. In Illustration 11, replacing the old soda machines with new ones did a great deal to build the collective morale of the workshop. Everyone was just a little more excited about being able to get a cold soda. But new soda machines did little to motivate anyone to increase their individual work performance.

2-2-11. Motivation is about what gets you and me up in the morning, and it's what causes us to go to the gym. Motivation moves us towards action and stops procrastination. Motivation is more about the reward; it is the carrot. We seek it out and it moves us toward a goal. If you want good grades (the carrot), you have to be motivated to do the work. You can have the best school environment with the highest morale in the country, but you have to be motivated to be part of that success.

2-2-12. In order to talk about motivation, you have to talk about the classic elements of reward and punishment: the reward (or carrot) versus the punishment (or stick). We all like the carrot, which comes in the form of positive reinforcement, and we typically want to avoid negative reinforcement, or the stick.

Positive Reinforcement

2-2-13. Positive reinforcement is just that: a positive reward for the actions and behaviors you want from whomever you are trying to motivate. Napoleon was credited with saying he could rule the world if he had enough ribbon. He was remarking on how much he admired the power of properly awarded ribbons and medals. Your job as a leader is to discover the best and most effective way to reward your team members for their efforts. The default answer might be money; money is a *prime* motivator for many people. You also might be surprised to find out that not everyone is motivated by money. You may be even more surprised to realize that there are studies that tell us that when money is the primary or sole reward, it can actually de-incentivize rather than motivate.

Money Does Not Motivate

In the *Journal of Vocational Behavior*, Timothy Judge and colleagues found that the association of money to job satisfaction is actually very weak. The authors reviewed over 120 years of research and 92 quantitative studies to verify this simple fact. These findings are not just true for the United States; they are true internationally as well.

The global research company Gallup reports annually on the state of the American workforce. In their report, you will find increasing trends that support the idea that money is not the primary motivator we assume it to be. Perks like flex time can be more important than money; 51% of people would change jobs for more flexible work hours. Employees are looking for perks like paid vacation, better saving programs, health insurance and paid sick leave.

People are also motivated by better working environments. They are often spurred on by what they see on television and in the movies regarding cool workplaces, like Google, Apple, Twitter, and other hipster tech and rising star companies. Free gym memberships, on-site daycare, cool flexible workspaces, and tuition reimbursement for increasing one's job skills, are all popular perks. Often these perk are less expensive in the long run than simply offering people more money.—*Illustration 12*

2-2-14. I worked for a Fortune 25 company after I separated from the military, and I was making a lot of money. Many times I had remarked as an officer that what I wanted out of a civilian job was to be rewarded based on my efforts. I wanted a job where the harder I worked was directly related to the amount of money I could make. I found that job and at first it was great. Soon, however, I found that I was burning out quickly and that money wasn't a primary motivator for me. My problem was I did not feel that what I was doing was making a difference. So I left to work for a nonprofit where I made less money but my happiness and motivation at work increased many times over.

2-2-15. Motivation can come in many different forms. I want to caution you, as a younger leader, about a one-size-fits-all motivational system. For example, some people will respond well to public praise while others will not. What you have to do is be creative and flexible. Pay close attention to your team and ask questions about what they'd like to see in the way of perks and recognition.

2-2-16. A quick comment on motivating volunteers. Many of you are currently or soon will be working with volunteers. Since money is obviously not a motivational tool for volunteers, you have to look at other factors. After 20 years of experience working with volunteers, I can say that volunteers primarily want three things. First, they want to be informed of the organization's goals and what the end result of their volunteer time will be. Second, they want to know you are listening to them and thus giving them a say in certain decisions. Third, they want to know that what they have done has made a difference in some way. Communicate these three items and your volunteers will stay motivated.

The Sharp End of the Stick, or Negative Reinforcement

2-2-17. The reality is that not everyone is going to perform to the standards set by you, their leader, or by the leadership above you. That means you have to deal with poor performance. Some people will require punishment as a response to not meeting the standard or the goals that have been established. Punishment is a way of motivating individuals *away* from the negative behaviors and back toward positive behaviors. It's important to remember that just one person can destroy your overall morale; it is your job to keep your people in check. The problems that arise can be as simple as not showing up on time or outright insubordination.

2-2-18. We will deal with the issue of solving worker performance in the next section, evaluation. For now, let's highlight a few areas of negative reinforcement you want to avoid so that you don't harm the overall morale of the organization.

   a) Avoid mass punishment. Seldom is everyone at fault and it is a morale killer.

   b) Avoid *threatening* punishment. It will make your team feel threatened from *within*, and with all the threats from outside the organization, no one needs to feel threatened from within the organization. Remember the power of trust and cooperation. Also, do not threaten punishment that you are not willing to follow up on. If you draw a line in the sand and tell your team that if they cross the line you will take specific actions, and then you do not take that action, you are telling them it is really okay to not meet your performance expectations. Do not make idle threats.

   c) Be consistent and treat everyone fairly.

d) Investigate not only the result of the problem but the *cause*. That team member who is always late may have an unavoidable reason for being chronically late. Help solve the problem rather than issue punishment.

2-2-19. In closing this section on morale, remember that morale is a *primary* leadership function. Morale and motivation are unquestionably linked and a great leader knows the importance of both. As the leader, first secure the overall morale of your organization. Without high morale, there is no motivation for the team to succeed, and little initiative to be productive or creative. High morale builds perseverance when things become difficult and challenging. It is the unit, team or organization with the highest morale that survives the most difficult times. High morale is what makes the most elite units so successful. Units such as the Army Ranger, Special Forces, and Navy Seal teams rely on their overall training, their pride, and their shared experience to build such a high level of morale that they can accomplish the seemingly impossible. With practice and intent, you too can build morale to this elite level.

Section Three

Evaluation

2-3-1. When we are defining evaluation, we use words like systematic, determination, judgment, assessing value, assigning merit, and overall worth to the cause. I doubt anyone ever looks forward to this kind of "evaluation." Who wants to be under this type of pressure?

2-3-2. Unfortunately, there are many companies that do see evaluations as a way of systematically, usually annually, assessing individuals in this punitive manner. The results of the corporate evaluation system are to destroy the motivation of individuals and the morale of the collective team. I have no intention of teaching you any evaluation system, not even the system used within the military. By the time I finished telling you how the military does evaluations, it is likely they will have already made revisions in an attempt to find a better way to meet the needs of an ever-changing military culture. It is also probable that whomever you take your first leadership position with already has an evaluation system in place and will expect you to learn it and use it.

2-3-3. Our goal here is to understand why evaluation is important, and to offer best practices to follow when using evaluations. As you lead yourself and others, evaluation is a necessary process for leaders marching forward. Evaluations done well increase individual and team productivity and assist in making sure we avoid repeating the same mistakes.

Self-evaluation

2-3-4. Before moving forward to evaluating your organization's team members, it is vital that you have done the necessary self-evaluation first. Back in section one, we talked about the four core principles to self-leadership. Number two was self-awareness (1-1-10). There, I briefly mentioned that you needed to be aware of your personal talents and strengths as well as your weaknesses. Most of us have a good grasp of our weaknesses. People have been pointing out our weaknesses and trying to fix them for years. What I want to focus on is evaluating your *core strengths*. What is it about you that is most natural to you?

2-3-5. You have a specific set of core strengths, and these strengths are unlikely to change much over time. Your areas of greatest strength are the activities where you have the highest degree of confidence in your success each time you perform in that specific area. Another way to identify your areas of greatest strength is to break them down into individual talents.

2-3-6. Talents are naturally recurring patterns of thought, feelings, behavior or attributes that can be productively applied. Talents are not knowledge or skill, or simply what you might be good at. Your talents are those things that you do *without any effort*. Talents are core to your personality. They are the things that might cause your parents to say: "I just don't know where she gets it." They remain constant in your everyday actions. Your talents empower you; they make it possible for you to reach higher levels of excellence and fulfill your potential.

2-3-7. You might be talented with numbers, and you might decide based upon what those numbers tell you. Maybe you are really good at listening, or at making friends. Do you love to read and seek out answers to unanswered questions? Perhaps you are great at anticipating what needs to get done or you are a list maker. You might even love speaking in public. All of these are indications of individual talents, and we all have different talents that make up our overall strength set. I've written an Amazon bestselling book: *Who's in Charge of Bob? The Key to Moving from Ordinary to Extraordinary*. This book is designed to assist you in directly identifying your individual talents. I would recommend that you pick up a copy of the book and then take a close look at your talents.

2-3-8. I also recommend that you take a talent/strengths assessment to help you identify your natural talents. The assessment that I personally recommend is the online Gallup Strengths assessment. It costs a few dollars, but it is the most respected tool and, according to my research, it provides you with the most detail of any of the assessments available. You can find the Gallup Strengths Assessment at www.Gallup.com.

There are two other assessments that I recommend: The Values in Action character assessment or VIA, and Marcus Buckingham's Standout assessment. Having taken all of them, I can testify that they yield similar results, but each assessment has a slightly different focus.

2-3-9. Apart from these assessments, a very simple way to begin to identify your personal talents is to ask those who know you best what they believe your talents are. Remember to employ good listening skills so you do not miss what they are saying. It can be a humbling experience to hear what others think you are good at, because we spend so much time in negative self-talk. To hear others praise your talents can be difficult, but don't dismiss what they are saying.. Also, you might be good at something but not realize it until others share what they think. On the other hand, you might think you are good at something when in fact you are not. Once you have identified your true talents, start investing in them so they become definite strengths.

Organizational and Team Evaluations

2-3-10. Evaluations are necessary, and critical for growth. Without evaluating our progress and setbacks, we cannot move our organization or individual team members forward. Too often, the focus of evaluations is on the negatives and not the positives. This makes the entire evaluation process unpleasant at best, and it can be counter-productive. But it does not have to be this way. As a leader you can structure an evaluation process that focuses on individual growth and potential.

2-3-11. With a little effort you can employ many of the following *best practices* in your leadership around evaluations. If you do, you can begin to shift the culture of evaluations. Take time to absorb the best practice elements of evaluation and use them with your team members. This will help build trust and cooperation, and will, in turn, increase commitment, loyalty, and morale.

Evaluation Best Practices

a) Evaluation should be *a continuous and consistent process*. Too often we only offer evaluation in the form of an official year-end evaluation summary. I promise that everyone, including leadership, hates doing these year-end evaluations, and yet we continue to do them. Stop now and start providing feedback continuously.

b) The goal of evaluations should be to move the individual and organization towards improvement, *to march forward*. People tend to live up to their leader's expectations, so let them know what they are doing right and where they could improve. Set high expectations and lead by example.

c) Acknowledge effort. This is critical considering our current working culture, which is not going to change anytime soon. Like it or not, those entering the workforce have lived under the concept that they should be rewarded solely for their effort. It is a byproduct of the "trophy generation" problem. Everyone was rewarded with a "trophy" regardless of their individual achievement or skill. Don't misunderstand my point. You should and need to acknowledge effort that is producing *positive results toward the goal*. You do not acknowledge or reward poor performance or below standard work. If you do, you will continue to receive poor performance.

d) Never allow obvious poor performance to continue. Stop it as soon as you become aware of it. Remember, bad news does not get better with time. It is much easier to adjust an individual's or team's performance along the way rather than after the fact.

e) Avoid public reprimand. No quality leader will publicly reprimand a subordinate. There is absolutely no need to humiliate anyone. The real result of a public reprimand is loss of respect for you as the leader. The exception would be in the case of safety. Always protect people first.

f) Listen, listen and listen some more. Listen to what your team is saying about how people are getting along.

Listen to how they feel about how the overall operations are running (morale), and how they feel about the goals being set. Listening will let you know how they believe the leadership is responding to issues that may be causing problems. Careful, this is not gossip time. You are not talking; you are listening.

g) Meet with your entire team and have them rate their own performance as a team. Then allow them to rate their own individual performance. Here is a tricky one: ask them then to score their peers. I would caution you about making this part of the public evaluation. However, it can reveal a great deal about how individual team members see everyone else's contribution to achieving the goals. In the Army, we do peer-evaluation summaries. There are actually elite units where the other members of the team can peer-evaluate a member out of the unit. This can be an unforgiving process, but you have to have the ultimate level of trust and cooperation within these units to accomplish the missions you are given.

h) When a project is ongoing over a long period of time, set predetermined times over the life of the project to evaluate the team's progress. I've sometimes been surprised to find out that an ongoing protect was not going as planned; yet, team members were reluctant to voice their concerns. They didn't want to rock the boat—which could be pointing to a leadership problem with a lack of trust and cooperation. Encourage your team to speak up when they see something going wrong. Again, bad news does not get better with time. Likewise, encourage your team to speak up when they see things going well. Some projects go much better than expected, and you should recognize these achievements.

i) Once a project is complete, do a *formal* after action review (AAR). I am constantly shocked at how often I am told by leadership that they do after action reviews only to find out they have done them poorly or they have not really done them at all. Sitting around the day after the project is over and patting yourself on the back for a job well done does not count as an after action review. Nor does gathering in a room trying to figure out what went wrong. Without a formal process, it can turn out to be just a complaint session.

A formal AAR takes planning and time. You have to gather everyone together and take the time to actually write down and *record* what you have accomplished, identify areas where you need to improve, and discuss what you will not repeat (good and bad) in the next project. This is also the perfect time to do the ongoing evaluations of your team members. Ask everyone to evaluate the overall project and their roles in its eventual success or failure.

I have attached as an appendix a formal after action review (AAR) sample. Please, as a young leader, take my advice when it comes to the power of doing formal AAR's. They will help take you from being a good leader to being an exceptional leader.

2-3-12. As we sum up evaluations, it is critical you recognize that evaluations are necessary if you plan to march your team forward towards success. Evaluations should not make your team member feel like he is being sent to the principal's office. As a young leader, change the punishment evaluation culture. Focus your attention on doing continuous and consistent evaluations throughout the year. During longer projects, take the time to schedule team and individual evaluations periodically to assess progress and problems. Start now to employ evaluation best practices into your personal leadership skill set.

Section Four

Shortening the Learning Curve

2-4-1. Why is asking for help so hard? Is it because society has made seeking help a sign of personal weakness? I believe that is exactly what has happened. Have we bought into the saying; "You learn more from failure than you do from success?" I do not know about you, but give me success every time. I want to avoid failure, and I can attest to the fact that you will learn more from your successes than from your failures. Plus, you only learn from failure if you take the time to evaluate all the areas that went wrong and then work toward a new solution. Unfortunately, we seldom do this, so we keep failing at the same stuff over and over. Asking for help and seeking advice is not a sign of weakness; it's a sign of *brilliance*.

2-4-2. Do not make mistakes you do not have to make. *Shortening the learning curve* is so much easier than trying to do everything from scratch. The best way to shorten your learning curve is to seek out advice and counsel from other people who are more experienced than you. As a young leader you will face problems you could never have imagined. The good news is that someone else has already been there and solved that problem. They have already made the mistakes that you will be prone to making. They have experienced most of what you will experience. So why would you not want to seek out their advice? Most people are more than willing to help you avoid major pitfalls if you will just ask for their help. You cannot be a pest though; there are some things you have to learn to work out for yourself. However, when you are faced with a difficult situation or problem with which you have no experience, be smart and seek advice.

2-4-3. You have grown up in a world where information is readily available: no books, no studying, and no experience necessary to solve both simple and highly complicated problems. The World Wide Web is available to you at your fingertips on your smartphone. Looking stuff up and gathering information has never been easier, and that is a good thing. In so many ways, readily available information has simplified our lives. Finding information that a decade ago would have taken hours, days, and perhaps even weeks to get is now a few taps away on the screen. But do not be fooled into thinking that access to information is the same as having someone teach you the information. There is a huge amount of detail and nuance lost in the raw information you can easily find.

2-4-4. Rapidly available information comes without personal experience or expertise, but there is no substitute for personal experience when it comes to learning a new task. YouTube videos are amazing at teaching you raw information, but I'd trade the video to have the hands-on training with the actual expert most every time. I want to encourage you not only to find the information but also to find *coaches* and *mentors* who can assist you in understanding how to apply the information.

2-4-5. Coaches and mentors are the perfect blend of raw information with personal expertise and the experience you need to shorten your learning curve as a young leader. Another way of looking at this is to remember that in order to *be in command* you must first learn to *come under command*. In this case you are coming under the command authority of a coach or mentor so that in the long run you can take command of yourself and others.

2-4-6. Coaching and mentoring are not the same thing. Both offer very different attributes and have immense value in shortening the learning curve. There will be times when you need both a coach and a mentor, or you may need one more than the other. Finding a coach is typically not that difficult; there are many coaches for hire and some businesses have a coaching program that you will be a part of. Often times these programs are labeled as mentoring programs but they are really coaching programs. Let's discuss the difference.

Defining Coach and Mentor

2-4-7. Coach: Coaching is more task and skill driven. It is about others having some sort of content expertise. A coach or a coaching program has very specific goals and is less relationship-oriented than mentoring. Coaches can be younger or older than you as long as they have the skill and/or knowledge set you do not have but need. Coaches can easily coach many people at the same time if they are focused on the same outcome. When we think of a coach or coaching program, most of us will envision a sports team; but you can hire personal coaches in almost every career field. Personal coaching is a multi-billion-dollar-a-year industry. In our society we are all doing more with time, and hiring a personal coach can reduce our learning curve and thus speed up our progress and success.

2-4-8. Mentor: Characteristically, mentoring is about a longer term relationship between individuals. One person seldom mentors large numbers of people at a time. Quality mentoring is typically about developing a relationship between two people. Some people believe and expect that they will become "friends" with their mentor. This may or may not be the case, but becoming buddies with your mentor does not equal success. Mentoring takes mutual trust and cooperation. If you want to be future-focused and deal with the whole person, then a mentor is what you need.

Attributes of Coaching and Mentoring

Coaching:

- Coaching is a formally structured arrangement with goals and objectives.
- Coaching is focused on improving performance in your position or job.
- Coaching has time constraints. When specific goals and objectives are set and then completed, the coaching stops.
- The coach's emphasis is on assessing, monitoring and adjusting the knowledge or skill level of the person being coached, with the goal of increasing performance.
- The person doing the coaching needs to have greater knowledge and experience than the person they are coaching.
- Often coaching is expected within the workplace as part of your job. Your immediate supervisor may be expected to train you in specific areas. Likewise, you may be expected to train the subordinates under you.
- The quality of coaching can greatly vary, especially within the workplace when coaching is expected. If you find yourself in a situation that isn't working, seek other counsel.

- Coaching can easily be done on the spot with immediate feedback.
- Coaches are expected to set the attitude within the relationship.
- Coaches are often available for hire and are subject matter experts.
- Teaching basic tasks is expected of a coach. More advanced training is found in the mentoring relationship.

Mentoring:

- Mentoring is more of an abstract relationship formed between individuals that have similar goals and objectives but vastly different expertise and experience levels.
- Mentors are often older than the individual being mentored because of the level of expertise required. However, experience and expertise is more important than age.
- Mentoring is focused on the individual, on assessing their overall needs, and on working towards improvement.
- Mentoring is a two-way beneficial relationship and will often extend beyond the working relationship.
- Mentoring requires a high level of trust between individuals. Mentoring seeks to develop not just specific job skills or enhanced knowledge; it also seeks to develop the entire person. Therefore, trust and honesty must exist within the mentoring relationship.
- Your mentor is not your best friend. You certainly should have a friendly relationship, but your mentor is seldom your best friend, so don't expect it.
- Mentors may have very little expertise regarding your specific industry. A mentor is concerned about provid-

ing overall wisdom and development in many areas, not just industry specific knowledge or skills.

"A coach has some great questions for your answers; a mentor has some great answers for your questions."—Unknown.

Lost in the Noisy World

When I decided to expand my work with students and become an inspirational speaker, there were two things I knew I was going to need.

First, I needed training, and I was going to need assistance navigating a new business model in an industry I knew almost nothing about. There is nothing easy about becoming a speaker; there is a huge amount to learn. Becoming a speaker requires building a personal brand, creating a platform, learning about whom to contact, developing relationships, and learning marketing techniques. I was going to need a coach and a coaching program to shorten my learning curve.

Finding a program where I could receive coaching on how to build a speaking business wasn't very difficult. I did some research and I asked a few other speakers in the youth market who they would recommend as a trusted source. Ultimately, I made an excellent choice. I selected a program that fit my budget and that provided me with all the basic information I needed to set up a speaking business. The program shortened my learning curve significantly.

Next, I needed someone in the speaking industry who could give me honest feedback and provide me with insight regarding how to better develop my own speaking strengths and how to manage my weakest areas. I needed a mentor.

Finding a mentor was much more difficult than finding a coach or coaching program. Mentoring is about developing a relationship, and relationships take time. About two years into developing the essential elements of my speaking business, I was lucky enough to build a relationship with another very successful youth speaker. He's *eighteen* years younger than me. That's right, eighteen years younger.

More often than not, a mentor is older than you, but it's certainly not a requirement. In my case, my mentor, Brooks Gibbs, had ten years of experience in the speaking industry that I didn't have. But I also had something to offer Brooks. Because I was older than him, I had educational and life experiences that he didn't have. So he and I were able to assist each other, which is another attribute of a quality mentoring relationship. Both mentor and mentee are getting something from the relationship.

What I know for sure is that without the coaching and mentoring from highly qualified people, I would certainly not have been as successful in the speaking industry. So my advice is to find both mentors and coaches throughout your working life.—*Illustration 13*

Section Five

The Resilient Leader

2-5-1. Resiliency is your capacity to recover from and deal with adversity or the difficulties in life. It is your ability to believe that things will be 'okay.' Some people seem to be naturally more resilient than others, but resiliency is still a skill that can be learned and invested in.

2-5-2. Resiliency is the heartbeat of the leader. It is the fuel that sustains you during times of difficulty. Resiliency holds all the other elements of your leadership abilities together. If you are not a resilient leader, and cannot march forward, how can you expect anyone on your team to follow your leadership? This may all sound harsh, and perhaps even unfair, but the truth has a tendency to be difficult. As the leader you are the one setting the example in all areas but especially when it comes to being resilient.

2-5-3. As a young leader I never heard the terms resilience or resiliency. I was trained under a hardcore, be tough, suck it up and drive on mentality. No whining or crying in the Army. Crappy stuff happens every day. It was a 'deal with it or get out of the way' style of leadership. This kind of be-tough attitude works on a surface level, but can it create long-term issues. Being a leader that can deal with difficult and trying times is not solely about being tough; it is about being resilient. Let's take a closer look at being a resilient leader.

2-5-4. Resilient leaders are individuals who have developed the ability not only to deal with difficult times effectively, but also to grow from the experience and thrive in the face of challenging circumstances. They learn to bounce back and assess where they can improve their ability to deal with any adversity they might face. Resilient leaders understand the cumulative effect that stress has on them and on their team, and they manage that stress. Not being able to realize the cumulative effect of stress and hardships is where the military's 'be tough and drive on' attitude falls short. In fact, the Army has in recent years devoted an immense amount of time and effort changing its attitude about what it means to be a resilient leader and soldier.

Embrace the Suck

Military training is difficult both physically and mentally; it's designed to be that way. Being a soldier and learning to lead others in the most highly stressful environments imaginable is the most difficult job in the world. It is one of the key reasons the military model of leadership is so efficient at training young people to be amazing leaders. Every soldier has to learn to perform under imminent stress.

The way I managed to deal with the stress of my military training was to tell myself to "embrace the suck." No matter how difficult the training was, I had to remind myself that it was all part of the process of becoming a better soldier and leader. The entire training process is designed to get you ready to perform under the great stress of deployment and combat.

Embracing the suck meant reminding myself that I was not the only one who was physically and mentally exhausted, hungry, and too hot or too cold. There is always someone to your left and your right enduring whatever hardship you are going through. This provides you with mutual support and camaraderie. It was important to remind myself that my instructors had once been right where I was, and that it was their job to make sure we were well trained and successful. The instructors don't get rewarded for failing everyone. Do not misunderstand me: often the initial phase of training, whether it is basic training, Airborne School, Air Assault School, or Ranger School, is designed to assess your desire to *be* there. If you are not mentally and physically ready, then you need to be someplace else, because you are a danger to yourself and others.

Embracing the suck meant keeping my attitude in check. Sometimes the best strategy is to see the absurdity of your situation and just laugh. Having a sense of humor allows you to release stress. I had to persevere with positivity and maintain an attitude that was optimistic. Sometimes it is the little things that help you get through a difficult situation; and finding the humor in any situation is what helped me. I always tried to remember that my instructors, once they were done giving me and my buddies hell all day, went home to their wives, kids, and dog. They had to change diapers, scoop the dog poop out of the yard, and do dishes just like everyone else.

So when life gets difficult, and it will, embrace the suck.—*Illustration 14*

2-5-5. Sense resiliency is about learning to deal with the difficult stuff in your daily life and to believe that things will be okay. How do we become resilient? It all starts with our attitude. Leaders understand the power their attitude plays in becoming resilient. In my first book, *B.A.S.I.C. The Student Leadership Field Manual*, I devote an entire section to the power of attitude. I encourage you to check it out.

2-5-6. A resilient attitude focuses on optimism. Optimism is about having a positive outlook regarding the future, and the possibilities that the future holds for you and your team as a leader. Optimism is a coping mechanism when life is difficult. However, for many people, being optimistic is much easier said than done. I believe that most people tend to be less optimistic about the future than ever before. I especially think this is true for young people in school and just starting their careers. The reason is simple; it is what we call *negative self-bias*.

2-5-7. Negative self-bias is the tendency to focus your attention upon the negative circumstances of your life rather than the positives in your life. Negative self-bias gets in the way of seeing the real potential you have. Negative self-bias is manifested in negative self-talk and sounds like this: "Things will never get any better;" "There's nothing I can do to change things;" "Nobody likes me;" I'm not good at anything;" or "I'm not good enough." These are only a few examples of how our negative self-talk gets in the way of us being optimistic and thus building resiliency.

2-5-8. Optimism is sometimes referred to as the "engine of resilience." We know that people who focus on being optimistic are happier and suffer less depression. Their health is generally better and they live longer. Who does not want to live longer? Having an optimistic attitude means you are more successful in school and work. You have stronger relationships and perform better under stressful situations. All this sounds like a reason to develop an optimistic attitude and therefore resilience.

2-5-9. Unfortunately, negative bias is a very strong force, and it often prevents us from being optimistic and therefore resilient. We tend to get stuck in the past and have difficulty seeing the potential in the future. But in order to be resilient we have to move forward. The Army uses the analogy of "Hut the Good Stuff," as a way of marching forward. The point is to focus on the good in any situation and to look toward the future by setting goals and rejecting negative self-talk.

2-5-10. Here are some specific ways you can focus on being a resilient leader.

- Have an attitude of gratitude. Be grateful for what you have. Stop looking to compare your life and current situation to others you think have their life all together.
- Resilient leaders resist negative self-bias in their personal life and at work. They set the example. If a leader is negative about what is going on and spends time complaining, it sets a bad example for the team. When you hear others using negative bias, see if you can redirect the negative into a solution that points toward a more optimistic outcome or future.
- Remember the iceberg analogy. When you see an iceberg floating along in the ocean, all you see it the "tip" of the iceberg. The vast majority of the huge iceberg is under water where you cannot see it. Just like people: what you can see on the outside is often a very poor reflection of what may actually be going on in their lives. This is especially important as a leader. A team member's poor attitude at work may have absolutely nothing to do with work and everything to do with what else is going on in their life. Do not assume what you do not know. Spend some time asking about how your team is doing, not just at work but in life. This will build trust and cooperation. If possible, and if appropriate, offer assistance whenever you can.
- Resilient leaders focus on their personal strengths rather than spending time trying to fix themselves or others. You certainly cannot ignore weaknesses, but rather than

trying to fix them, learn to manage them. Then you will have a lot more time to develop not only *your* personal strengths, but also those of your team.

- Set realistic and attainable goals and celebrate your wins. Too often leadership will set goals that everyone knows are not attainable. This will feed into your team's negative bias. As the leader, if you find yourself facing what seem to be unattainable goals, set intermediate goals that are attainable. This will keep you and your team focused on the possibilities rather than on failure.

- Build relationships outside of your organization. If you are leading a team and you only have relationships within your organization, you never get any "down time." You have to have other relationships that have no connection with your leadership life. I have personally made this mistake, and it is a resiliency killer.

- Before becoming a speaker and author, I was so connected with my work and leading others that I started to lose my sense of identity, and it ultimately had a negative effect on my leadership ability. Fortunately, I had a friend who helped me to see where my current behavior was leading me. He suggested I needed a hobby, something new to focus on other than work. He suggested I try fly fishing, and now I'm addicted (in a good way) to the art and sport of fly fishing.

- Resilient leaders evaluate past and present circumstances to identify areas that may be creating unnecessary stress within their team. This takes practice but as a leader you always need to be assessing how your team is reacting to whatever may be causing difficulty.

- Resilient leaders understand that there are times when members of your team can become toxic to its overall success. Individuals that focus on the negative and cannot seem to adjust their attitudes sometimes have to go. It's called *tough empathy*. You can understand a team member's issues, and their pain, and you can sympathize with their personal situation. However, as a leader, your job is to accomplish the mission, task, and goals set before you and your team. No one likes to be the bad guy and be in the position where you have to let someone go, but it comes with being a leader.

- Being flexible is key to being a resilient leader. If you are rigid and inflexible you are going to make your own leadership life difficult. Situations can change every day, so you always have to be flexible. In the Army we have a saying: "improvise, adapt, and overcome." A resilient leader is a flexible leader.

- Resilient leaders do not *give the power over their attitude away*. In my keynotes and workshops, I talk about what it means for you to give the power of your attitude away, and I use the following example:

  I ask audience members to raise their hand if they are grudge holders. Not surprisingly, more than fifty percent of my audience members raise their hands. Then I simply ask them why they are willing to allow someone else to control how they think and feel. If you hold a grudge against someone, you are giving *them* power over your attitude, so stop and let it go. Resiliency is a byproduct of your attitude. You cannot be resilient if someone else is controlling your attitude.

2-5-11. Let me say it again: resiliency is the heartbeat of the leader. It is fuel that sustains you during times of difficulty. Resiliency holds all the other elements of your leadership abilities together. The resilient leader has command over their attitude, and they do not give that power away. Being a resilient leader means you actively take time to develop the skills of resiliency; you fight against the forces of negative bias and keep an optimistic outlook. Resilient leaders march themselves and their teams forward into the often unknown and difficult future with confidence.

Summary

I want to conclude *Leaders Marching Forward: The Advanced Student Leadership Field Manual* with a singular but immensely important statement: **Lead by example.**

When you get right down to the very core of leadership, and what it takes to lead others, it is really about leading by example. People pay more attention to *what you do* than anything you might say. So never ask anyone you are leading to do what you have not already done, are not currently doing, have not trained to do yourself, or are not willing to do. The very best leaders always lead by example.

All of the advanced leadership skills we have discussed are skills that can be learned, invested in, and ultimately mastered. As a young leader, you must invest in developing your leadership skills. Those that actively seek to continually improve their leadership skills will set themselves apart from others. You will quickly move from being an ordinary leader to an extraordinary leader.

Always continue to march forward.

Appendix

After Action Review (AAR) Sample

Here is a sample of the information that an AAR is trying to collect. This example will work well for student leaders putting on an event. Also, the AAR can be expanded or reduced based on your specific needs.

Before the Event

Event Title/Theme:

What is your primary goal for the event?

Finances: (pay close attention to these records)

Budget

Expected income and payments

Dates:

Include the start date and closing date.

Include important dates such as leadership team arrivals and departures.

Deadline dates including all registrations.

Alternate dates, if available, for "rainouts."

Times:

Start and end times

Place:

Physical location of the event, address, phone numbers

Contact Personnel:

Collect the title of the individual(s), their name, address, and office and cell phone numbers.

Collect the names of anyone you speak to that is a decision maker.

If you are inviting guests, speakers or presenters, collect all of their info.

Contracts:

Get everything in writing. A verbal promise is not enough.

Create an email folder and keep all email correspondence.

Keep all contracts on file.

After speaking with someone on the phone who agrees to do something or provide you with something, create a summary email of the conversation and send it to yourself and the person you spoke with.

Number of people expected to attend: and number actually in attendance.

Personnel List:

List all your team members and their responsibilities.

Supplies:

Listing your necessary supplies is often a step that is missed. This step will save you lots of time and headaches, because every year you think you will remember the stuff you need, but you never do. Have each member of your team create their own list and also consolidate your lists. Your supplies list will grow to the point where you eventually have everything you need listed.

After the Event

Ask yourself and your team to consider the broad questions: What did we do right? What did we do wrong? Ask these questions for each of the areas below. As the leader, you need to listen closely to the answers your team gives you.

Finances:

Did you stay within your budget?

List both savings and unexpected costs.

Where could you have saved money? Where should you have spent more money?

Did you collect the expected income from your registrations?

Should you increase or decrease the cost of the event?

Event Theme:

Was your theme appropriate? Did your audience "get it"?

Did you achieve your primary goal?

What worked and did not work as far as achieving the goals you had set?

Was it fun? What could you do to make it better in the future?

Should you do the event again? Why or why not?

What goals should you set for next year that you might have missed out on this year?

Dates:

Was the date you selected appropriate?

Did it conflict with other events that drew attendance away from your event?

Was the day of the week the best one possible for your audience?

If you changed the date/time of year, would you increase attendance?

Did you receive your registration on time? If not, why, and can you improve on this?

Times:

Did you start and end on time? Why or why not? Can you improve on this?

Should you consider changing the time of events to better serve your audience?

Place:

Was the location appropriate for this event?

Did the location people fulfill their contract? Do you need to add (or subtract) elements of the contract?

Was the location too small or too big?

Did they have the necessary supplies and equipment for your needs? (stages, sound and video equipment, rooms, tables and chairs)

Did your attendees enjoy the facilities?

Did the event host at the location treat you and your attendees well?

If you were satisfied with the location, have you booked your next event?

Supplies:

What did you forget?

What did you bring that you did not need?

What would be a 'nice to have' in the future?

Review of Team Members:

In general, did the team get the job done as expected?

Did you have everyone you needed? If not, who do you need to add?

Did you have too many people?

Did everyone have a job?

Did your team do their individual jobs? If not, how do you plan to deal with that?

How did they do their jobs? List areas of improvement and point out successes.

Did anyone try to 'steal the show' by putting themselves above the goals of the event?

After Action Reviews (AARs) are very specific to the event and to the information the leader is trying to collect. You may choose to focus on the overall success of the event; or perhaps it would be more helpful to focus on the job performance of individual team members. Or maybe you need to pay particular attention to the "beans and bullets" of the operation. As the leader, you decide on the goal of any AAR that you do.

One Last Story
Talking My Way into College

I have been fortunate throughout my life to be surrounded by amazing people who have provided me with amazing advice and leadership.

Upon graduating high school, I had no opportunity to get into college. I just barely graduated high school (2.12 GPA) and didn't have the academic scores to qualify for admission to college. However, I wasn't going to let that stop me from trying. So I applied to one school and didn't get in.

When I received their rejection letter, I picked up the phone and called the Dean of Admissions and told him I was not accepting the school's rejection of my application. The Dean was totally silent on the other end of the phone.

Then he stated: "Mr. Grooms, if you received a rejection letter, it means you don't meet the minimum requirements for admission."

"Dean, you're stuck on 'no'...How do we get to the yes part of this conversation?"

To make a long story short...he agreed to meet with me and talk about my admission. I wanted to get into the developmental studies program, designed for people just like me. The professor who was the head of the department would have to authorize my admission. She wasn't impressed with me at all. She said 'no' to my request to enter the developmental studies program. Honestly, I was pissed because I felt she was being dismissive of me.

I asked her what her problem was. "Why won't you let me at least try?"

She said dismissively, "Because you won't make it!"

My response, in a raised tone of voice: "You want to bet?"

That response actually worked. I think she was so surprised at my response she couldn't do anything but let me in to prove me wrong. I literally talked my way into college.

This professor was my advisor for the rest of the time I was in school, and she stayed on my case constantly. I was in her office over and over explaining any kind of "hiccup" in my grades. She insisted I improve in every subject area. She wanted nothing less than what she believed my best could be.

She even required me to *retake* a writing and grammar class that I passed because *she believed* I could do better. I really thought her goal was to get me to quit, so I had to retake the class.

I did do better and that meant I did better in all my other courses as well. She was right; I could do better. But I still was convinced that her goal was to get me to quit.

As you can imagine, we were not each other's biggest fans. I'd daydream about taking her out with my car. *Don't misunderstand me*; I'm only joking. Besides, I didn't want to kill her or anything horrible like that. I just wanted to knock her down really hard. Maybe just bump her by opening my car door as I drove by? But I'm sure she would have bounced right back, and I'd still be standing in her office trying to explain myself.

In the end, the result was that Dr. Colbert, my nemesis, never accepted anything less than what she believed was my best work. Looking back, as is turns out, she wasn't my nemesis after all. She was my number one ally. I'm confident that without her investment in my education, I would not have graduated college.

I graduated from the leading senior military college in the nation—North Georgia College, now called the University of North Georgia—as a distinguished military graduate and with a degree in business management, holding a 3.32 GPA. I received a commission as an officer in the United States Army. Not too bad for a kid who wasn't going to be able to make it.

This story isn't just about what I accomplished. It's about my learning to come *under* command before I could *be* in command. It's about perseverance and grit, and about never listening when other people put me down or when I got caught up in my own negative self-bias. It's really about all the people who invested in me, like my parents, my teachers who would give me just a little more flexibility when I needed it, and would also give me a ton of grief when I was slacking off. It's about having coaches and mentors that shared their wisdom, experience and knowledge. This story is about learning to manage weaknesses, focus on personal strengths, and the willingness to ask for and then accept help from others.

This story can be your story; a story of personal growth and leadership. Don't allow your, or anyone's, negative bias be the lead in your personal story. Maintain a positive outlook, hut the good stuff in your life, and seek help whenever you need it.

March forward into your future.

Thank you for investing in me.—Fred

About the Author

Fred Grooms is a popular inspirational speaker for student, adult, and corporate audiences. He is an educator, a three-time Amazon bestselling author, and an expert in the field of leadership and character education. Fred has over 20 years of experience teaching students how to identify their gifts, build character, overcome any limitations, and recognize their personal and professional call to leadership.

Fred sees his success as a direct result of learning the foundational elements of leadership taught in the military. As a cadet in the leading Senior Military College in the nation, the University of North Georgia, he developed his personal leadership skills and strengths and learned to manage his greatest weakness—his dyslexia. Upon graduating, Fred earned a commission as an officer in the U.S. Army. Since leaving the army, Fred has travelled throughout the U.S. speaking to students and many other audiences about leadership, resiliency, character and life skills.

Much of Fred's spare time is spent working as a volunteer, training service dogs for individuals with disabilities. If he is not on a speaking tour, you will find Fred working with a dog on its training goals or camping and fly fishing on the banks of a remote river.

You can find Fred Grooms on the Internet at:
www.fredgrooms.com
fred@fredgrooms.com

50816317R00070

Made in the USA
San Bernardino, CA
04 July 2017